starting out in
bridge

PAUL LAMFORD

Published by Everyman Publishers plc, London

First published 2001 by Everyman Publishers plc, Gloucester Mansions, 140A
Shaftesbury Avenue, London WC2H 8HD

British Library Cataloguing-in-Publication Data
A catalogue record of this book is available from the British Library.

ISBN 1 85744 287 3

Distributed in North America by The Globe Pequot Press, P O Box 480, 246 Goose
Lane, Guilford, CT 06437-0480.

All other sales enquiries should be directed to Mindsports, Everyman Publishers plc,
Gloucester Mansions, 140A Shaftesbury Avenue, London WC2H 8HD
Tel: 020 7539 7600 Fax: 020 7379 4060
email: dan@everyman.uk.com website: www.everyman.uk.com

To Emmalene Murphy

The Everyman Mindsports series was desgined and developed by First Rank Publishing

Typeset by Games and Pastimes Consultancy, London (gampas@aol.com)
Production by Book Production Services
Printed and bound in Great Britain by The Cromwell Press Ltd, Trowbridge, Wiltshire

Contents

Introduction

Bridge has been around in some form for over 100 years, and the game from which it developed, whist, for maybe four times as long. In 1886 John Collinson published a pamphlet entitled *Biritch*, a form of Russian whist, and this is clearly the forerunner of auction bridge.

The game as we know it was really created by Harold S Vanderbilt on the *SS Finlandia* on a winter cruise in 1925-26. It received worldwide publicity in a famous challenge match between Ely Culbertson and Sidney Lenz in December 1931 and January 1932. Bridge made the front pages of many of the world's broadsheets, and bridge columns appeared regularly thereafter. Further less welcome publicity was given to the game in 1959 when the British pair, Terence Reese and Boris Schapiro, was accused of cheating during the World Championship, allegations that were never proven. Nowadays, there are maybe 50,000,000 players worldwide, of whom about one million play the game seriously. Perhaps the best known player is the actor Omar Sharif who has done much to popularise the game. It is increasingly being taught in schools, and yet is also regarded by American psychologists as a means of preventing senility among older people; a game for all ages.

The purpose of this book is to teach the basics of the game using the Acol bidding system, used by the vast majority of British players, and by an increasing number of players worldwide. The book is ideally suited to be used in conjunction with a bridge course, or as a self-tutor. Exercises at the end of each chapter are designed to test the reader's understanding of the material. Of course, there is no substitute for competitive practice, and the many Internet servers provide online play for the keen beginner wishing to improve.

The author would like to thank Stefanie Rohan for editing and proofreading and Byron Jacobs for suggesting this title and a companion one on backgammon. Any comments or corrections should be sent to the author at gampas@aol.com.

In this book we have adopted the principle of referring to North and South, or a declarer, as 'he' and East and West, or a defender, as 'she'.

Chapter One

The Basics

- **The Rules of the Game**
- **Procedure**
- **The Bidding**
- **The Play**
- **No-trump Contracts**
- **Suit Contracts**
- **Try it Yourself**

The Rules of the Game

Bridge is a partnership card game for four players played with a normal pack of 52 cards, without the jokers. It is is a 'trick-taking' game, and a trick comprises one card from each of the four players, always contributed in a clockwise direction. Each trick is won by one side or the other according to simple rules.

Partnerships can be mutually agreed, or each player can cut a card, with the two players cutting the highest cards being partners and sitting opposite each other. The cards are shuffled and each player draws one card. The person who draws the highest card deals first and is known as the dealer. The cards are again shuffled and cut, and then dealt one at a time to each player, starting with the player on the dealer's left, until each player has 13 cards and the pack is exhausted.

After the deal, each player picks up his or her hand and sorts it into suits, in the order spades, hearts, diamonds, clubs, as in the following illustration. The ace ranks high, then king, queen, jack, ten, nine, etc. down to two.

The hand is sorted as shown

The hand should be concealed from the other players. You may prefer to alternate the red and black suits.

Procedure

There are two stages to a hand of bridge; the auction and the play. In the auction the object is to announce how many tricks you and your partner can take together. In addition, this is the stage during which any trump suit, which we shall explain shortly, is selected. The auction starts with the dealer and rotates clockwise until there is no further bidding in that, after any bid, three people pass consecutively. The last bid prior to these passes becomes the final contract.

After the bidding has finished the hand is then played by the person known as the declarer. This is the player who first bid the suit in which the contract is to be played. The person to the left of the declarer makes an opening lead by placing one card face up and then the dummy is placed face up on the table by the partner of the declarer as illustrated below:

The dummy is laid face up on the table

NOTE: The declarer selects and plays the cards of the dummy as well as choosing cards from his own hand, but the defenders play their own cards separately

If the four cards of a trick are all of the same suit the highest card wins. The winner of the trick turns it face down in front of him and then leads a card to the next trick. If a player does not have a card of the suit led, he may trump with a card of the trump suit and thus win the trick. This is also known as ruffing. If a further player also does not have the suit led he can play a higher trump and win the trick. A player who does not have a card of the suit led may, instead, discard a card from another suit — he is not obliged to trump.

There is one type of contract, in no-trumps, where, if you cannot play the suit led, you cannot trump the trick but have to discard another suit.

At the end of the play the total tricks made by each partnership are added and compared with the number announced in the bidding. If the partnership made at least as many tricks as they bid, they are said to have fulfilled their contract. If they made fewer tricks, they have been defeated.

The Bidding

This is sometimes known as the auction and begins with the dealer and then rotates clockwise. The minimum number of tricks you can bid for is seven and you do this by opening one of a suit or One No-trump. This means that you think you can take seven tricks to the opponent's six and the suit you nominate will be the trump suit. Each bid means that you think you can make six tricks plus the number you call. So a bid of three spades means you think you can make nine tricks, and spades will be the trump suit.

The order of the bids is important. The lowest bid you can make is One Club, the next highest is One Diamond, then One Heart, then One Spade, then One No-trump. The order, clubs, diamonds, hearts, spades, no-trumps, stays the same throughout the auction and you will need to remember this order. The highest bid you can make is Seven No-trumps which means you think you can take all thirteen tricks.

You don't have to make a bid — you can also say pass. If all four players pass, the hand is 'thrown in' and a new deal takes place. The two other calls you can make are double and redouble which we will deal with in a later chapter. You must always make a 'call' of either pass, double, redouble, or a higher bid than the previous one.

The Play

After the player to the left of the declarer leads a card and the next player puts down the dummy, the declarer then decides how to play the hand. He is trying, first of all, to make as many tricks as he said he would in the bidding. If you have played whist before, this part of the game will be easier for you than the bidding and you will soon pick it up. The difference from whist is that all three players can see the fourth hand (the dummy), so each player can see 26 cards. Here are example hands at both no-trumps and trumps:

No-trump Contracts

The South hand is the dealer (we usually refer to the four players by the points of the compass for ease of recognition).

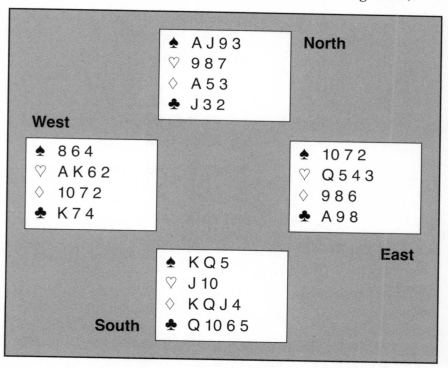

He opens One No-trump and everybody passes. West decides to lead the ace of hearts and places it face up in the centre of the table. At this point North places his hand face up as dummy. Traditionally, South now says, 'thank you, partner,' and sets about trying to make his contract.

TIP: The first stage is to count how many tricks you can make in total without losing the lead

In spades declarer has four tricks, none in hearts, four in diamonds, and none in clubs. This totals eight, so as soon as he gets the lead he will be well-placed. In fact, as we shall see in the play, the defenders can take the first six tricks, so that in practice the declarer can only make seven tricks.

Now cross off the cards, or deal them yourself and play them out one by one, to see how the play would go. The card that wins each trick is shown in bold. In each case the card led to that trick is given first.

Trick 1:   ♡**A**, ♡7, ♡3, ♡10

Trick 2:   ♡**K**, ♡8, ♡4, ♡J

Trick 3:   ♡2, ♡9, ♡**Q**, ♣5
(South could not follow and there are no trumps, so he has to discard)

Trick 4:   ♡5, ◇4, ♡**6**, ♣2
(South has to discard from his hand and from the dummy)

Trick 5:   ♣4, ♣3, ♣**A**, ♣6

Trick 6:   ♣8, ♣10, ♣**K**, ♣J

Trick 7:   ♣7, ♠3, ♣9, ♣**Q**

Trick 8:   ♠**K**, ♠4, ♠9, ♠2

Trick 9:   ♠**Q**, ♠6. ♠J. ♠7

Trick 10:   ♠5, ♠8, ♠**A**, ♠10

Trick 11:   ◇**A**, ◇6, ◇J, ◇2

Trick 12:   ◇3, ◇8, ◇**Q**, ◇7.

Trick 13:   ◇**K**, ◇10, ◇5, ◇9

So the declarer wins seven tricks and the defenders win six tricks. South is therefore successful in his contract of One No-trump. At the end of the hand, the score is recorded, which we will explain in a later chapter. The cards are collected and shuffled prior to the next deal. Usually two packs of cards are used, so that dealing of the next hand can take place while the previous pack is being shuffled.

Suit Contracts

In our next hand East is the dealer and passes. South opens One Heart, West passes and North bids Three Hearts. Why does North go higher even though his partner made the first bid? As we shall see in the next chapter, you want to bid as high as you can, as there are bonuses to be gained from making contracts above a certain level. East passes and South bids Four Hearts. Then the next three players pass, so that Four Hearts becomes the final contract. South is thus trying to make ten tricks with hearts as trumps.

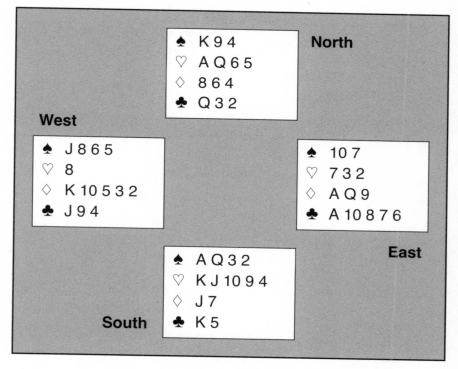

West selects the three of diamonds for her opening lead, and again North places his hand face up. Traditionally, the trumps are placed on his right, or the declarer's left, but otherwise the dummy is laid out as on page 7. Again you count how many tricks you are certain to make before you start the play. In spades you have three, in hearts five, in diamonds none and in clubs one. This totals only nine and you need to make ten tricks. As we shall see in the play, one more can be achieved by ruffing a spade with one of dummy's trumps.

The defence begins with two diamond winners. South trumps the third round of diamonds, and then plays the high trumps.

TIP: It is usually correct to draw the opponents' trumps in a suit contract

Later the declarer makes tricks with the high spades and a club trick by giving up a trick to the ace of clubs.

Again we go through the play card by card:

Trick 1:   ◇3, ◇4, ◇**A**, ◇7

Trick 2:   ◇**Q**, ◇J, ◇2, ◇6

Trick 3:   ◇9, ♡**9**, ◇5, ◇8
 (South does not have a diamond, so he can play a trump and win the trick)

Trick 4:   ♡4, ♡8, ♡**A**, ♡2

Trick 5:   ♡**Q**, ♡3, ♡10, ◇10
 (West does not have a heart, and they are trumps, so she has to discard)

Trick 6:   ♡5, ♡7, ♡**J**, ◇K
 (The king of diamonds may seem a large card to discard, but South has already trumped diamonds)

Trick 7:   ♣K, ♣4, ♣2, ♣**A**

Trick 8:   ♣6, ♣5, ♣9, ♣**Q**

Trick 9:   ♠**K**, ♠7, ♠2, ♠5

Trick 10:   ♠4, ♠10, ♠**Q**, ♠6

Trick 11:   ♠**A**, ♠8, ♠9, ♣7
 (East does not have any spades, but she has no trumps either, so she has to discard)

Trick 12:   ♠3, ♠**J**, ♡6, ♣8

Trick 13:   ♣3, ♣10, ♡**K**, ♣J

South makes ten tricks, and therefore succeeds in his contract of Four Spades.

These two contracts were selected so that the play was relatively straightforward. In Chapter Eight we will give some more examples of declarer play. At this stage, count your tricks, draw trumps and play on your longest suit first.

Try it Yourself

Exercise 1: Decide whether the final call is allowed in the following sequences. (C stands for clubs, D for diamonds, H for hearts, S for spades and NT for no-trumps)

a) Pass — Pass — 1NT — 1C
b) 1D — Pass —1H — 2S
c) 2S — 2NT — Pass — 3NT
d) 1H — Pass — 2H — 1NT

Exercise 2: Which card wins the trick in no-trumps in each of the four following tricks? The card led is given first

a) ◇J, ◇10, ◇Q, ◇9
b) ♡2, ♠7, ◇A, ♠8
c) ♣5, ♣8, ♣3, ♡10
d) ◇7, ♣8, ◇10, ♣A

Exercise 3: Which card wins the trick with hearts as trumps in each of the following tricks? The card led is given first

a) ♡Q, ♠7, ♡J, ♣A
b) ◇A, ♡2, ♡6, ◇Q
c) ♣10, ♠4, ◇6, ♣Q
d) ◇J, ◇Q, ♡2, ◇A

Exercise 4: When is the dummy placed face up on the table?

a) before the bidding takes place
b) at the end of the bidding after three players in a row pass
c) after the opening lead has been made
d) after the first trick has been played

Exercise 5: Which of the following statements are true and which are false?

a) The person who makes the first call is the dealer.
b) If the first three players pass, that is the end of the bidding.
c) The highest bid that you can make is Thirteen No-trumps.
d) The dummy is always the partner of the declarer.

Solutions are on pages 121-4.

Chapter Two

Principles of Bidding

- **Hand Evaluation**
- **The Opening Bid**
- **The Response**
- **Game and Slam Contracts**
- **The Overcall**
- **Doubles and Redoubles**
- **Try it Yourself**

Hand Evaluation

The easiest way to evaluate a hand is by way of a system called high-card points. You count only (at this early stage) the aces, kings, queens and jacks in the hand and you assign the following values for them:

> Ace = 4 points
> King = 3 points
> Queen = 2 points
> Jack = 1 point

The following hand therefore has nine points:

> ♠ K 9 4 3
> ♡ Q 8 3
> ◇ K J 2
> ♣ 10 8 2

Three points are in spades, two in hearts, and four in diamonds.

The Opening Bid

In the first chapter you had no benchmark to decide whether you should make a bid. It should be noted that you can open the bidding with any hand, under the rules of the game, but the usually accepted minimum requirement to open the bidding at the one-level is 12 points. This means you have an above average hand because there are 40 points in the pack and, on average, each player receives ten points.

As you shall see shortly, you can also add points to the hand depending on the number of cards in your longest suits. Usually you open with a bid of one, which means that you are initially aiming to take seven tricks. You also nominate as trumps the suit of which you have the most cards.

Here is an example of a correct opening bid of One Spade:

> ♠ A Q J 9 6
> ♡ K 8 3
> ◇ Q J 2
> ♣ 6 4

This hand has 13 points (seven in spades, three in hearts, three in diamonds and none in clubs).

The Response

When your partner opens the bidding, you then evaluate your hand with the knowledge that he or she has at least 12 points. Consequently, you need much less to bid in response. Here the traditional requirements are reduced to only six points. Opposite the opening bid of One Spade which we gave on the previous page, it is correct to respond One No-trump on the following hand:

♠ 3
♡ J 9 6 4
◇ K 9 4 3
♣ Q 8 7 3

The above are only examples of an opening bid and a response. There are established guidelines for selecting the suit and level during the auction, and these will be dealt with in this book. Indeed, you do not usually respond on six points if partner opens One No-trump. You must ask yourself what you are trying to achieve in the bidding. Primarily, you are trying to make at least as many tricks as you bid. The reason you bid higher is that you earn bonuses above a certain level.

Game and Slam Contracts

Why do you need to bid when your partner opens the bidding? Firstly, you may not have many of the suit he chose as trumps and you can suggest another trump suit or no-trumps. Secondly, and more importantly, you score extra points for bidding and making the following contracts:

Three No-trumps

Four Hearts

Four Spades

Five Clubs

Five Diamonds

These are all known as game contracts and receive a bonus which is explained in more detail in the section on scoring. There are also even larger bonuses for bidding and making 12 tricks or 13 tricks. These are known as slams (small slams for 12 tricks and grand slams for 13 tricks).

This is where the hand evaluation above, which assigns a number of high-card points to each hand, is important. Over the years the average number of points to achieve each of these contracts has been determined and is as follows:

Three No-trumps, Four Hearts or Four Spades	**25 points**
Five Clubs, Five Diamonds	**29 points**
Six of anything	**32 points**
Seven of anything	**37 points**

What you are trying to achieve in the bidding, therefore, is to go as high as possible, but not too high. If you do not make the number of tricks for which you bid, then the opponents score points, and these are called penalties. As you will find in later chapters, the number of high-card points you hold is crucial and you are always trying to tell your partner, but only by what you bid, how good your hand is. Bidding is a conversation between you and your partner, where every bid tells the other a little bit more about your hands. You start by bidding your longest suit and you should be thinking about the number of points to reach the various bonus levels. Usually if you bid a level higher you are showing a stronger hand. If you look at the hand at the bottom of page 15 opposite the hand on page 16, the bidding should stop after the first hand opens One Spade and the second hand responds One No-trump. Why? Because both hands are near the minimum required to open and respond. If you were to bid again on the first hand you would be showing a stronger hand, or one unsuitable for no-trumps.

This discussion has oversimplified the principles of bidding and we will look at the range of points shown by various bids in the next few chapters. As you would expect, it is difficult to express your hand exactly in one bid. When you open one of a suit, you say that you have at least 12 points and at least four of the suit bid. Is there an upper limit? There obviously needs to be otherwise your partner does not know whether to bid any higher. This limit is usually 19 points, although some hands which open at the one-level have a little more, between 20 and 22 sometimes. If you have six points, therefore, you should respond to your partner because between you there may be enough points to make a game contract.

The Overcall

When the opponents open the bidding, the person making an opening bid has at least 12 points. However, there is a total of 40 points in the pack, so this does not preclude the opponents from bidding. On many hands, both sides can make more than seven tricks, depending on which suit is trumps. It is important, therefore, to make a bid when you have a reasonable hand, and the accepted minimum for an overcall is ten points and always a five-card suit, although, as we shall see later, we may sometimes have fewer. An example of a One Spade overcall, over an opening bid of One Club, One Diamond or One Heart:

♠ A Q J 9 2
♡ K 8 3
◇ J 4 3
♣ 9 5

Your partner will assume you have at least ten points and at least five spades for this bid. If the opponents opened One Spade, however, you would pass. Often you need to bid at a higher level than the opponents, because the opening bid was in a suit which outranked yours, or because an opponent opened One No-trump. As this will necessitate your bidding at the two-level, the requirements are increased to 12 points, or ten points with six cards in the suit: For example, you would overcall One Spade with Two Clubs on the following hand:

♠ 7
♡ K J 6
◇ 8 5 3
♣ A Q 10 9 4 2

However, if the two of clubs were the two of any other suit, it would not be a sound two-level overcall.

Doubles and Redoubles

So far we have only looked at bids which are a combination of a number and a suit or no-trumps. However, as we mentioned in Chapter One, there are two other bids you are permitted to make according to the Laws of Bridge, the double and redouble. These are often difficult for beginners to understand, but it is important to introduce them at an early stage. To learn bridge without them would be equivalent to learning golf without using a sand wedge.

A player may double the last bid made by the opponents, even if this has been followed by two passes. If three people then pass in succession, the auction ends and the contract is played in the last bid, but doubled. This has no effect on the play, but the score achieved is substantially altered. For instance:

One No-trump—Double—Pass—Pass—Pass

The auction has now ended and the final contract is One No-trump doubled. This still means the declarer has to make seven tricks. If he succeeds he will earn more points, if he fails he will lose more points. If there is a bid after the double, then the double does not carry forward and is effectively cancelled. A redouble can be made if the opponents' last call (other than pass) was double:

One No-trump—Double—Redouble—Pass—Pass—Pass

Again the contract is One No-trump, but this time it is doubled and redoubled. Again declarer has to make seven tricks. The score for being successful is increased further, while the penalty for failing is likewise increased.

What is the purpose of these doubles and redoubles? Well, if you bid too high, the opponents may elect to double the final contract, and if it fails, the penalties are increased. The points scored are also increased if you succeed, but the opponents will not usually double a contract unless they expect to defeat it. The redouble can be used when the opponents wrongly double a contract which you expect to make.

In the early days of contract bridge the double and redouble were mainly used to increase the scoring, with both sides offering their opinions on whether the final contract would be successful. However, bridge players soon found that there was a better use for the bid of double, especially when used after the opponents opened at the one-level, when you are unlikely to have enough strength to defeat the opposing contract. Consequently, the double came to be used on hands that could not make an alternative bid, and partner was expected to bid in response, the so-called take-out double. In Chapter Five we shall look at how you can use the double on hands on which you would otherwise be awkwardly placed.

Try it Yourself

Exercise 6: You are dealer. How many high-card points do you have and what would you open?

♠ 9
♡ A Q J 8 6 3
◇ K Q J 2
♣ 8 4

Exercise 7: Your partner is dealer and opens One Diamond and the next hand passes. What do you bid with this hand?

♠ J 7 4
♡ Q 8 3 2
◇ 9 4
♣ 10 7 6 3

Exercise 8: The lady on your right deals and opens One Diamond. What would you bid on the following hand?

♠ K 6
♡ A 5
◇ J 9 5
♣ K J 10 5 3 2

Exercise 9: The man on your right deals and opens One Heart. What do you bid on the following hand?

♠ A J 9
♡ K J 8 7 2
◇ 5 4
♣ Q 10 8

Exercise 10: Your partner deals and passes, and the lady on your right opens One No-trump. What do you bid on the following hand?

♠ K Q 7 6 4 2
♡ A 10
◇ 4
♣ Q 8 6 4

Chapter Three

The Opening Bid

- **One No-trump**
- **One of a Suit**
- **Refining the Point-Count**
- **Two of a Suit**
- **Two No-trumps**
- **Two Clubs**
- **Three of a Suit**
- **Three No-trumps**
- **Higher Bids**
- **Try it Yourself**

One No-trump

As we mentioned earlier, most hands that are suitable for an opening bid are started with one of their longest suit. However, one bid at the one-level is used to show what is called a balanced hand, with a specific range of points.

A balanced hand is one with at least two cards in each suit, and ideally without two suits each containing only two cards. The accepted distributions for a balanced hand are usually as follows:

4-3-3-3

4-4-3-2

5-3-3-2

In Britain particularly, and sometimes in parts of Europe, the normal range of points for opening One No-trump is 12-14 and this is the range we shall adopt for this book. It is often referred to as the 'weak no-trump'.

The following three hands are all correct One No-trump openings:

a)
    ♠ A K 4
    ♡ Q 8 3 2
    ◇ 9 4
    ♣ A 7 6 3

b)
    ♠ Q 10 8 7
    ♡ J 9 8 6
    ◇ A K 5
    ♣ Q 2

c)
    ♠ 6 5
    ♡ K Q J 3
    ◇ 8 7 5
    ♣ A K 5 4

Some teachers would advise their students not to open One No-trump on the last hand as there are two suits without a high card. This is poor advice. The opening bid of One No-trump tells your partner two things, that you have a balanced hand and that you have 12, 13 or 14 points. You should use it when you can.

If you have five cards in spades or hearts (known as the major suits) whether or not to open One No-trump depends on the quality of the suit. The simplest rule is to open One No-trump unless your suit contains two of the top three honours, when you should bid the suit. This hand, for example, is an acceptable One No-trump opening bid:

d)
    ♠ J 10 8 6 4
    ♡ A 3
    ♢ K Q 2
    ♣ Q J 4

However, the distribution on which you should not generally open One No-trump is 5-4-2-2. On the following hand the better opening bid is One Heart:

e)
    ♠ 5 2
    ♡ J 9 6 3 2
    ♢ A K J 2
    ♣ A 4

One of a Suit

If a hand does not fulfil the requirements for an opening bid of One No-trump, and has between 12 and 19 points inclusive, then the player should open at the one-level in his longest suit. We will look shortly at what to do with hands of 20 points or more. On the following hand you would open One Diamond, your longest suit. Although it is a balanced hand, it has 16 points, too many for you to open One No-trump.

    ♠ K 5 3
    ♡ A Q 2
    ♢ 9 8 3 2
    ♣ A K 5

Even though the diamond suit does not have any honour cards, it is still correct to start with one of that suit. As we shall see later, if partner responds, you can make a second bid, and this will be in no-trumps, to show that you have a balanced hand. When you have two or three suits of equal length, then you need to apply some rules to decide which suit to open.

Firstly, with two five-card suits, open the higher suit. On this hand, for example, you open One Heart:

♠ K 5
♡ K J 9 5 2
♢ 8
♣ A Q 10 8 5

The above rule applies even with five spades and five clubs.

When you have two four-card suits, then you open the lower. On the following hand, therefore, you would open One Club:

♠ A K 9
♡ K 10 8 6
♢ A 2
♣ Q J 5 2

Finally, you may have three four-card suits. The best way of expressing the rule for how to handle such hands was given by Michelle Brunner in her book, *Bridge with Brunner*. With a red singleton, open the suit below the singleton (the suit in which you have only one card). On this hand open One Diamond:

♠ Q J 9 2
♡ J
♢ K 10 9 4
♣ A K 5 2

With a black singleton, open the middle of the three four card-suits. With this hand you open One Heart:

♠ K J 8 3
♡ A K 5 4
♢ Q J 4 2
♣ 9

The above rules need to be studied carefully. Making the correct opening bid provides the basis for a good auction.

So far, you have only counted the high-card points for a hand, using the 4-3-2-1 system mentioned in Chapter Two. We will now look at distributional points which can be added to a hand for extra length in suits, and also a few deductions which should be made for adverse features:

Refining the Point-Count

Additions
After you have totalled your high-card points, you should then

also consider whether you have any distributional points.

If the hand is one of the balanced patterns on page 22, then there are no points to add. Indeed, a point should be deducted for having the shape 4-3-3-3, as the absence of a second four-card suit is a disadvantage. However, if you have a less balanced hand, then you will be opening one of a suit, and can add the following distributional points:

a) for a five-card suit and a four-card suit, add one point

b) for two five-card suits, add two points

c) for a six-card suit, add one point

d) for a six-card suit and a four-card suit, add two points

e) for a six-card suit and a five-card suit, add three points

f) for a seven-card suit, add three points

g) for a seven-card suit and a four-card suit, add four points

The requirement for opening the bidding in a suit at the one-level is that the total of high-card points plus distributional points is 12 or more. Some hands with a seven-card suit will open at a higher level, as you will see later in this chapter.

The following hand merits a two-point addition, for a six-card suit and a four-card suit, and can be counted as 12 points and is a sound opening bid of One Spade:

$\spadesuit$ A J 10 8 6 4
$\heartsuit$ 3
$\diamondsuit$ K Q 9 3
$\clubsuit$ 8 7

NOTE: It should be stressed here, that you can only apply an addition for one of a) to g) above. Hands with eight-card suits or longer are very rare, and they will be dealt with later

Deductions

We mentioned above that the balanced shape 4-3-3-3 is a disadvantage and you should deduct one point for that holding. The other deductions you should make are for singleton honours. For a singleton king, queen or jack, you should deduct one point, although you may add that point back in later if partner bids the suit. A singleton ace is a minor flaw, so do not deduct anything for that. The other defect a hand may have is containing the honours in the short suits. If less than half the points are in the two longest suits, then deduct a point. Take the following hand:

♠ K Q
♡ Q 8 7 6
◇ J 5 4 3
♣ A 8 5

There are no added points for this hand, as the shape is balanced. Indeed, nine of the 12 points are in the two shortest suits and one point is therefore deducted. The correct opening bid is therefore to pass.

Two of a Suit

At the start of the section 'One of a Suit', we indicated that all hands with 12-19 points which were not balanced should be opened one of the longest suit. The reader might assume that hands with 20 or more points are opened at a higher level. This is only partially true. Some such hands are, provided they fit certain requirements. Others are still opened one of a suit.

To open a hand with two of a suit, the main requirement is that you would expect to make a game contract when partner has a hand that will not respond to an opening bid at the one-level. You must also have at least a good five-card suit. For example on the following hand you should open Two Hearts:

♠ A 3
♡ K Q J 7 6 5
◇ A K Q 6
♣ 3

Including distribution, where you add two points for a six-card suit plus a four-card suit, this hand is worth 21 points. More importantly, you expect to make at least eight tricks with hearts as trumps. You can count one in spades, five in hearts (after a trick has been conceded to the ace) and three in diamonds, a total of nine. If partner has, for example, the king of spades, or even just the jack of diamonds, you are likely to make game in hearts. If you open One Heart, partner will pass with only the king of spades. If you open Two Hearts, partner is obliged to respond, in the manner which we will explain in the next chapter. However, without a good five-card suit or a

balanced hand you should open at the one-level on hands with
20-22 points:

> ♠ A K J 4
> ♡ A K Q 9
> ◇ K
> ♣ Q 9 8 7

There is no choice here but to open One Club. This hand does
not fit the requirements for any of the two-level opening bids.

The opening bids at the two-level showing eight sure tricks can
be made in diamonds, hearts or spades. We shall look shortly at
the opening bid of Two Clubs, which is a special bid, showing
23 or more points, or a certain game in one's own hand. The
other bid at the two-level is Two No-trumps:

Two No-trumps

Just as the opening bid of One No-trump shows a balanced
hand, so does the opening bid of Two No-trumps. Similarly it
shows a specific point range, most often played as 20-22 high-
card points. This is the range we will adopt for this book. An
example of an opening bid of Two No-trumps:

> ♠ K 6 4
> ♡ A Q J 9
> ◇ A J 4 2
> ♣ A Q

It is quite acceptable to have five-cards in hearts or spades
when opening Two No-trumps. Having a singleton, even if it an
ace, is regarded by most experts as unacceptable. Furthermore,
the distribution 5-4-2-2 is often opened Two No-trumps, and a
six-card club suit is also acceptable, as the opening bid of Two
Clubs is a special bid as we shall now see.

Two Clubs

This is our first example of an artificial bid — one that doesn't
promise at least four cards in the suit that has been bid. All
other opening bids at the one- or two-level are 'natural' bids.
The bid is 'forcing', in that partner has to respond regardless of
his hand. The requirements for an opening bid of Two Clubs
are either of the following:

i) 23 or more high-card points, or

ii) the virtual certainty of being able to make game regardless of the strength of partner's hand.

Two examples of an opening bid of Two Clubs:

a)
  ♠ A K J
  ♡ K Q 10 9
  ♢ A K 4 2
  ♣ A Q

This hand has 26 high-card points. It is a balanced hand, but you do not open Two No-trumps, as that bid shows 20-22 points. You open Two Clubs, intending to rebid no-trumps.

b)
  ♠ A K Q J 9 3 2
  ♡ K Q 8
  ♢ K Q 2
  ♣ None

This hand has only 20 points but is very likely to make Four Spades, and may well make a higher contract. It should therefore be opened Two Clubs.

c)
  ♠ K Q J 10 9 4
  ♡ K Q J 9 3
  ♢ A 2
  ♣ None

The above hand, however, whilst almost certain to make game, is best opened with Two Spades. Partner is obliged to respond, as we will see in the next chapter, and you will then bid your hearts. With a strong two-suited hand, it is better to start by bidding one of the suits at the two-level, as that gives you the chance to bid the other suit on the next round.

Three of a Suit

You might think that it would be extremely rare for someone to start off with an opening bid as high as three. After all, it commits the person making the bid to try and make nine or more tricks without any knowledge of his partner's hand.

Indeed, being dealt a hand where you can be sure to make nine or more tricks is quite rare, and these hands are usually opened with one of the two-level opening bids above.

The opening bids at the three- and four-levels are known as pre-emptive bids. They are always made on hands with a single long suit traditionally of at least seven cards and **fewer than 10 high-card points**. Indeed, when making the bid the player is not expecting to succeed in his contract. That will depend entirely on how good a hand his partner furnishes.

The purpose of a pre-emptive bid is mainly to make life difficult for the opponents, who may have enough points between them for game, but have to start the bidding at an uncomfortably high level. A good example of an opening bid of Three Spades is the following hand:

♠ Q J 10 9 5 3 2
♡ 6
♢ 7 4
♣ Q J 10

This hand would expect to take about six tricks with spades as trumps, and yet the correct opening bid is Three Spades. It only has six high-card points, plus three for distribution. However it lacks **defence** in that it is not going to take many tricks if the opponents are playing a contract, particularly in a red suit. The opening bid of Three Spades is designed to make life difficult for them.

What are the requirements for an opening bid at the three-level. Firstly that depends on the vulnerability. This is a term which is new to readers and needs to be explained. If either partnership has already scored a game, then it becomes vulnerable. This will be clearer to you after you read the section on scoring on page 117. The effect is that a pair who is vulnerable on a particular deal will concede a higher penalty if the declarer fails in his contract. They therefore need to be more conservative in the bidding. You therefore have two benchmarks for an opening bid at the three-level:

a) **vulnerable:** the ability to guarantee six tricks

b) **non-vulnerable:** the ability to guarantee five tricks

These requirements are accepted by most modern players, although more conservative teachers would advocate seven tricks and six tricks respectively. The other recommended requirement for an opening bid at the three-level is that you hold at least three of the five honours in the suit.

Three No-trumps

This is a special bid which we will just mention at this stage for completeness. As hands that can guarantee nine tricks in no-trumps are opened with the bid of Two Clubs, this bid shows seven or eight cards in a minor suit, headed by the top three honours, and no more than a queen in the other three suits. It is often called the gambling Three No-trumps. Until you gain more experience you may decide not to employ it, and it is something of a *rara avis*. An example of a suitable hand:

♠ J
♥ 6 4
♦ J 10 7
♣ A K Q J 9 7 4

Higher Bids

It is rare that either side opens the bidding at the four-level or above, but such bids are still pre-emptive, showing a seven- or eight-card suited headed by at least three honours.

The requirements to open at the four-level are basically one more than those to open at the three-level:

a) **vulnerable:** the ability to guarantee seven tricks

b) **non-vulnerable:** the ability to guarantee six tricks

For an opening bid of Five Clubs or Five Diamonds you can add one further trick to the requirement. This would be an acceptable opening bid of Four Spades, vulnerable:

♠ K Q J 9 8 6 5 3
♥ 7
♦ 9
♣ 7 4 2

An example of an opening bid of Five Diamonds:

♠ 4
♥ K Q
♦ K Q J 10 8 7 5 4 2
♣ 10

Note that this hand has eleven high-card points, and could be opened with One Diamond. However, when you are dealt a nine-card suit, it is best to get in as high a bid as possible.

Try it Yourself

Exercise 11: You are dealer. What would you open on the following hand?

♠ K J 9 4 3
♥ A 10 7 5 4
⋄ K 2
♣ 8

Exercise 12: You are again dealer. What would you open on the following hand?

♠ K 5
♥ Q 10 6
⋄ A 9 5
♣ K J 10 6 4

Exercise 13: The dealer on your right passes. What would you bid on the following hand?

♠ Q J 8 3
♥ A J 9 7
⋄ 9
♣ K Q 5 3

Exercise 14: The man on your right deals and passes. What do you bid on the following hand?

♠ A 6 5
♥ A 9
⋄ Q J 10 8 6 5 4
♣ 3

Exercise 15: You are dealer. What is your opening bid?

♠ K Q J 6
♥ A K Q J 7
⋄ K Q 3
♣ A

Chapter Four

The Response

- **Responding to One No-trump**
- **Responding to One of a Suit**
- **Responding to Two of a Suit**
- **Responding to Two No-trumps**
- **Responding to Two Clubs**
- **Responding to Pre-empts**
- **The Opponents Intervene**
- **Try it Yourself**

When partner opens the bidding you are much better placed. If partner opens at the one-level, you know partner has a minimum of 12 points and if partner opens at a higher level you also know a great deal about partner's strength. This chapter covers the responses you make to the opening bids in the previous chapter.

Responding to One No-trump

Although you saw in Chapter Two that you can make a response with six points, when partner opens One No-trump there are two major differences:

a) Partner can have no more than 14 points.

b) Any bid you make has to be at the two-level.

TIP: Consequently, when you have a hand of ten points or fewer without a five-card suit, you pass when your partner opens One No-trump

The above is an important tip. The combined assets of the partnership are no more than 24 points and therefore you have fewer than the number of points needed for game, as explained in Chapter Two.

Weak Hands

We state 'without a five-card suit' in the above tip. If you do have a five-card suit then the hand will normally play better in that suit, as partner will, on average, have three cards in the suit as well. If the suit is diamonds, hearts or spades and you have fewer than 11 points, you should bid the suit. For example on this hand you respond Two Hearts:

♠ J 5
♥ J 10 9 8 6 2
⋄ 4
♣ 10 6 5 3

'A poor hand with only two points', you say, 'and I am being told to bid at the next level.' That is right, but the bid of Two Hearts is **a command for partner to pass**. It is sometimes called a weak take-out, but can have up to ten points. The only requirement is that the person making the bid thinks that it is better to play in a suit than no-trumps.

You may have wondered why you were advised to bid this way only if your suit is diamonds, hearts or spades. The reason is that Two Clubs is used as an artificial bid known as the **Stayman Convention**. It asks partner to bid a four-card heart or spade suit if he possesses one.

Strong Hands

When you have 11 or more points you should bid. What you do depends on whether you have a balanced or unbalanced hand and what you hold in hearts or spades (the major suits).

a) With a balanced hand without four or more of a major suit, you raise partner as follows:

i) 11-12: raise partner to Two No-trumps

ii) 13-18: raise partner to Three No-trumps

iii) 18-19: raise partner to Four No-trumps
This is invitational; partner passes or goes to Six No-trumps

iv) 20-22: raise partner to Six No-trumps

v) 23-24: raise partner to Five No-trumps
This is forcing; partner bids Six or Seven No-trumps

You may notice the peculiar change at the end, where you go back down from six to five. The reason is that when you bid five, you are saying you can definitely make six, and may be able to make seven. Partner must choose.

b) With a balanced or unbalanced hand with four of a major suit, you use the **Stayman Convention**. This asks partner to bid hearts or spades is he has four cards in that suit. For example:

♠ K Q 6 4
♡ A 9 5
◇ A J 9 7 5
♣ 4

Despite having only one club, you would respond to One No-trump with Two Clubs, the Stayman Convention. If partner has four spades, then you want to play in Four Spades because you have an unbalanced hand. If not, you will just have to take your chances in Three No-trumps and hope partner has some high cards in clubs.

If partner does not have four hearts or four spades, then he must respond to the Stayman Convention with Two Diamonds. If partner has both hearts and spades, then he will bid Two Hearts. You would then bid Three No-trumps, but partner can go to Four Spades as he would know the following tip:

TIP: If you use the Stayman Convention and then bid Three No-trumps, you must have a four-card major suit

If you had four hearts you would have supported partner. If you didn't have four spades, you wouldn't have used Stayman.

c) With an unbalanced hand and a five-card major suit, bid three of the major suit. On the following hand you should bid Three Hearts:

> ♠ 9
> ♡ J 10 9 7 4
> ◇ A Q 6 2
> ♣ A 5 3

The hand is too strong to bid Two Hearts, which commands partner to pass. Three Hearts **forces partner to bid,** which may get you a little high if partner has only 12 points. *C'est la vie.* Indeed, as you progress in bridge you will encounter different and more accurate ways to bid hands such as this, often employed by your opponents. These are not necessarily a good substitute for the simpler methods of bidding you will learn in this book.

d) With an unbalanced hand without a four-card or five-card major suit, this depends on the strength of the hand, and the distribution.

If you have 18 or more points, including distribution, then you may look for a slam, and the best method to force partner to bid is to jump to the three-level in a five-card minor suit. For example, on the following hand, you would respond to One No-trump with Three Diamonds, a forcing bid.

> ♠ None
> ♡ K 6 4
> ◇ A Q J 10 8 5
> ♣ A K 4 2

It is quite likely that you can make a slam in diamonds, or possibly in clubs. Force partner to bid again by jumping.

Sometimes you will just be looking for the best game contract. On the next hand you would respond to One No-trump with Three Diamonds again:

♠ None
♡ A 6
♢ Q J 9 5 3 2
♣ K J 10 9 6

The hand is unsuitable for no-trumps. You should bid Three Diamonds, and after partner's next bid, jump to Five Clubs. Partner will choose between playing in Five Clubs and Five Diamonds.

This concludes our discussion of responding to One No-trump. As you know partner's point-count fairly accurately, it is a lot easier to judge how high to go.

Responding to One of a Suit

When partner opens One Club, One Diamond, One Heart or One Spade, his hand is less well-defined than when he opens One No-trump. You know that he has at least 12 points, and no more than 22 points. Usually he will not have more than 19 points. You also know that the suit bid is partner's longest, or equal-longest suit.

Your first question is whether you have enough points to respond. As we stated in Chapter Two, you need a minimum of six points to respond, and should always do so when you hold those six points.

Before you decide how many points you have, you need to decide whether you have any extra points. In addition to the points for length that we mentioned earlier, you can add points for shortage, if and only if you have four or more of the suit which partner opened. The normally accepted additional points for shortage are as follows:

For a doubleton	**One point**
For a singleton	**Two points**
For a void	**Three points**

As the names suggest, a doubleton is only two of a suit, a singleton is only one of a suit, and a void is none of a suit. Don't forget that in order to add these points you need to have four of the suit partner opened or three of the suit partner overcalled or rebid.

If you have five of partner's suit, or if partner's bid shows five of his suit (for example an overcall) and you have four, then you can increase these shortage points as follows:

For a doubleton	**One point**
For a singleton	**Three points**
For a void	**Five points**

Pass

If you still have fewer than six points you will pass. On the following hand if partner opens One Heart you should pass:

♠ J 7 6
♡ Q 8 7
♢ J 9 7 5
♣ 10 4 3

If you have six or more points, the next question you ask is whether you have four of partner's suit and, if not, whether you have a balanced hand. If you have either of these then nearly all the time you will be able to describe your hand with a limit bid, but first we must mention a special bid:

The Pre-emptive Raise

The immediate raise to four of partner's major suit shows a distributional hand with about 3-9 high-card points, with five cards or more cards in partner's suit. This would be a good example of a raise of One Spade to Four Spades:

♠ Q J 7 6 2
♡ 5
♢ 8 2
♣ K 10 8 7 6

This hand has only six high-card points, but is still worth a raise directly to game. Even if you fail in your contract of Four Spades, it is quite possible the opponents could have made a contract in one of the red suits.

Other Responses

It is important here to distinguish between limit bids and other bids:

NOTE: A change of suit by the responder is an unlimited bid and forces the opener to bid again

However there are a number of bids which are limit bids showing a specific number of points. When we respond to an opening bid in no-trumps or when we raise partner's suit one or two levels, we are making a limit bid.

a) 6-9 points
If you have four of partner's suit and 6-9 points including distribution you can raise partner one level. This is one of the limit bids.

On the following hand you would raise One Diamond to Two Diamonds.

♠ 7 2
♡ K 7 5
◇ Q 10 9 7
♣ J 6 4 3

The hand has seven points (including one point for the doubleton) and is therefore in the range 6-9. This is a limit bid and all limit bids are non-forcing. Partner will only bid higher if he thinks it is right to do so.

If you do not have four of partner's suit, then you should either bid a new suit at the one-level or bid One No-trump. You should not, however, bid a new suit at the two-level, as this promises 10 points. On the following hand you would respond to One Diamond with One Spade:

♠ 9 8 7 2
♡ 8
◇ K 7 5
♣ A 8 7 5 2

Note that you are not responding in your longest suit here.

TIP: It is better to respond One Heart or One Spade when you hold four of that suit, in preference to bidding no-trumps or raising partner's opening bid of One Club or One Diamond

Responding One No-trump suggests a balanced hand, but does not guarantee it, as there are some hands with 6-9 points on which it is the only possible bid. For example, you would respond One No-trump to One Spade on this hand:

♠ J 7
♡ K 8 6 4 2
♢ Q 8 6
♣ J 3 2

This is a balanced hand, and again you do not have enough points to bid Two Hearts. Changing the two lowest clubs to diamonds however, gives you an unbalanced hand:

♠ J 7
♡ K 8 6 4 2
♢ Q 8 6 3 2
♣ J

On this hand you have no choice but to respond One No-trump despite having a singleton. The alternative is to pass, but partner might have 19 points, and you would certainly miss a game contract in that case.

If you have an unbalanced hand with three of partner's suit, then you should prefer to raise partner one level rather than bid One No-trump. Changing your last hand slightly, you would raise One Spade to Two Spades with the following hand:

♠ J 7 2
♡ K 8 6 4 2
♢ Q 8 6 3
♣ J

Bidding Two Spades is much less of a lie than One No-trump which *suggests* a balanced hand.

b) 10-12 points:
Again you ask yourself the question, 'do I have four of partner's suit?' If the answer is yes, then you can raise partner two levels. We use the word can, as it is still better to respond One Heart or One Spade with four of that suit, than to raise partner's One Club or One Diamond opening bid to three. For example:

♠ K 6 4
♡ A 5
♢ K J 8 6
♣ 10 9 7 2

If partner opens One Diamond, then raise to Three Diamonds. However, make a small change to the hand:

♠ K 6 4 2
♡ A 5
◊ K J 8 6
♣ 10 9 7

Now it is better to respond One Spade to One Diamond.
The second question to ask is: 'do I have a balanced hand?' If
so, then you can respond Two No-trumps. Again we use the
word can, as you would still prefer to make a response of One
Heart or One Spade.

On the next hand, if partner opens One Diamond, you should
respond Two No-trumps, showing 10-12 points:

♠ K 4 3
♡ Q J 8
◊ K 8 7 2
♣ Q 10 4

Changing the hand slightly:

♠ K 4 3 2
♡ Q J 8
◊ K 8 7
♣ Q 10 4

and now it is better to respond One Spade to partner's opening
bid of One Diamond.

When you have 10-12 points you are able to bid a new suit at
the one- or two-level, but you still bid your longest suit first,
and at the lowest level possible. On the next hand you would
respond to an opening bid of One Diamond with Two Clubs:

♠ Q 7 6
♡ 5
◊ A 8 4
♣ K Q 9 8 6 3

**NOTE: Responding Two Hearts to One Spade promises five
hearts. Responding Two Clubs or Two Diamonds only
promises four cards, or very occasionally three**

c) *13-15 points*:
When you have 13 or more points, you know that you will want
to play in a game contract. However, there is no need to
immediately bid a game contract on every hand. If partner has

a strong hand, you may make a slam. Generally you will respond with your longest suit at the lowest available level.

When you have four of partner's suit, you might think that you would raise partner three levels, but this takes up too many levels of bidding and stops your own exchange of information. When you have four of partner's suit, therefore, you just bid your longest other suit at the lowest available level, and then bid game in partner's suit on the next round.

WARNING: Do not raise partner to four of a major suit with 13-15 points. This is a pre-emptive bid, as shown on page 37

For example, partner opens One Spade and you have the following hand:

♠ K J 9 6
♡ 5 2
♢ K Q 4
♣ A Q 8 2

You should just bid Two Clubs for now, and partner is obliged to make another bid. You can then bid Four Spades. You might have to bid a three-card suit when you have a hand that is too strong to make a limit raise.

With 13-15 points and a completely balanced hand, you can respond Three No-trumps to any opening bid. The following hand would be a good example:

♠ A J 4
♡ K Q 9
♢ 6 5 3 2
♣ K J 5

If partner opens One Diamond, despite your having four-card support the correct response is Three No-trumps.

If you cannot make a limit bid, just respond in your longest suit at the lowest level. Partner's next bid will describe his hand further and you will then know how high you should bid.

d) *16+ points*

When you have 16 or more points and partner has opened the bidding, you can start thinking about a slam. However, it normally pays to start the bidding slowly, again bidding one of your longest suit. If you have 16 points including distribution, and either a very good suit of your own, or a fair suit and support for partner, then you can jump a level to tell partner this. If partner opens One Club you would jump to Two Spades on this hand:

♠ A K Q 10 6 2
♡ A 4
◇ 6 4
♣ Q 4 3

This tells your partner that you want to play in game, are interested in slam, and have a very good suit, or a fair suit and support for partner. With the latter, you will support partner's suit on the next round.

TIP: Do not overuse this jump bid. If you have a balanced hand or two or more four- or five-card suits it is best to start off with your longest suit at the lowest level

Responding to Two of a Suit

When partner opens Two Diamonds, Two Hearts or Two Spades, he is showing a good suit and at least eight tricks in his own hand. The first point to make is that however weak your hand you have to respond!

WARNING: However bad your hand, you cannot pass when partner opens at the two-level in a suit.

Even though partner has not opened Two Clubs, you may still be able to make game. Take the following hand:

♠ 3 2
♡ 8 7 6 5 3
◇ 4 3
♣ 9 7 6 5

This hand is a genuine Yarborough, named after the wily Duke of Yarborough who offered odds to all-comers against a hand of 13 cards containing no card above a nine. Unfortunately for the punters, the odds he offered were 1,000 to 1 instead of the correct 1,827 to 1. This represented a margin approaching 50% — very similar to the National Lottery.

It certainly is tempting to pass when partner opens Two Spades, but my hand on the occasion my student did was:

♠ A K 7 5 4
♡ K Q J 10 5
◇ A K 6
♣ None

I was successful in my contract of Two Spades (indeed I made an overtrick) but I would also have been equally successful in a contract of Six Hearts. The point is that an opening bid of two of a suit does not preclude having a second suit.

When you have 0-6 high-card points, and partner opens two of a suit, then you make a negative response of Two No-trumps if you have two or fewer of partner's suit. If you have three or more cards of partner's suit then with 0-3 points you can raise partner to three, with 4-6 points you raise partner to game.

With more than six points, you can also raise partner to three if you have three-card support or better, so that this bid is ambiguous and your later bidding will clarify which you have.

You can also bid a new suit, called giving a positive response, with at least a five-card suit headed by two of the top three honours. An example of a positive response of Three Diamonds to an opening bid of Two Spades:

♠ 6 3
♡ 8 2
◇ K Q J 8 4
♣ K 9 7 2

Jumping to Three No-trumps shows a balanced hand with 7-9 points, something like the following hand in response to an opening Two Spades:

♠ 5 3
♡ K 3 2
◇ Q J 8 5
♣ Q 10 8 7

Responding to Two No-trumps

We retain the same order as the previous chapter for the responses. The opening bid of Two No-trumps shows 20-22 points, but, unlike the other opening two bids, does not force you to respond. You therefore pass with 0-3 points as, on average, you are short of the 25 points required for game.

With a balanced hand of between four and nine points you just raise to Three No-trumps. You have enough for game but not enough for slam. With 10-11 points and a balanced hand you raise to Four No-trumps. This is an invitational bid which asks partner to go on to Six No-trumps with 21 or 22 points.

With 12-14 points you go directly to Six No-trumps and with 15-16 you again go to Five No-trumps inviting partner to bid Seven No-trumps with 21 or 22 points. With 17 or more you bid Seven No-trumps.

So you can see that you are adding partner's points to your own and judging how high to go.

This is fine for a balanced hand. However, it is much tougher to bid unbalanced hands. One useful gadget is the response of Three Clubs, which is like the response of Two Clubs to an opening bid of One No-trump. It is again the **Stayman Convention**. It asks partner to bid a four-card (or longer) heart or spade suit. On this hand you would bid Three Clubs in response to Two No-trumps:

♠   Q 10 6 2
♥   J 9 7 4
♦   K 9 8 2
♣   8

Partner will then bid a major suit, or respond Three Diamonds if he does not have four hearts or four spades. You can select the best game contract in each case.

You use the Stayman Convention only if you have one or more four-card major suits. If you have a five-card major suit, and have at least four points, you should bid the major and partner will act accordingly. For example:

♠   K J 10 6 2
♥   3
♦   Q J 8
♣   10 8 7 5

You would respond to Two No-trumps with Three Spades, showing a five-card suit and at least four points. All bids at the three-level in response to Two No-trumps are forcing. Similarly you can bid a five-card diamond suit, but you usually do this only when you have enough points to consider a slam, or when you are very unsuitable for no-trumps. A response of Four Clubs is used to show a good club suit, as the response of Three Clubs is the Stayman Convention.

Finally, if you think you know the correct contract, you should just bid it straight away. On this hand you should respond to Two No-trumps with Four Hearts:

♠ 8
♡ Q J 8 7 6 5 3
♢ 8 6
♣ 9 5 2

All game bids in response to Two No-trumps should end the auction.

Responding to Two Clubs

As you saw earlier, the Two Club opening bid is artificial and forcing, showing 23 or more points or an almost certain game in one hand. There is a conventional response to this which shows 0-6 points **or a hand unsuitable for any other bid** and that is Two Diamonds, often called a negative or waiting response. You would respond Two Diamonds on the hand just above and on the following hand:

♠ 10 9 8 5
♡ K 8 7
♢ J
♣ J 10 8 7 4

Again the bid is artificial and says nothing about your holding in diamonds. Partner will then describe his hand further as explained in Chapter Six on the opener's rebids.

When you have seven or more points you can make a positive response. With a balanced hand with 7-9 points you respond Two No-trumps and with a balanced hand with 10-12 points you respond Three No-trumps. The other bids you can make are positive responses in a new suit. If you have seven or more points and a five-card suit headed by two of the top three honours, you can bid the suit. If that suit is diamonds, you need to bid Three Diamonds, as Two Diamonds is the negative response above. Here is a good example of a positive response of Two Spades to an opening bid of Two Clubs:

♠ A Q J 8 6
♡ Q 2
◇ 8 5 4
♣ 9 7 3

Responding to Pre-empts

When partner opens the bidding at the three- or four-level, he was intending to make life difficult for the opponents. Sometimes, however, he makes it difficult for you. You have fewer options opposite a pre-empt. You can pass, raise partner to game, or bid Three No-trumps, if partner has opened at the three-level. The other possibility is to bid a new suit. It is important to remember the following rule:

WARNING: If you bid game in no-trumps or a new suit opposite a pre-empt, that is a command to pass. If you bid a new suit which is not game, then partner must bid again

For example, say partner opened Three Spades as dealer, and you have this hand:

♠ A 9
♡ 5 4 3
◇ A K Q 7 4 2
♣ A 5

You would respond Four Diamonds, and partner would have to bid again and show any additional feature of his hand, either showing a singleton, or an ace or king in a side suit, or supporting your suit, as appropriate.

If partner opens Three No-trumps or a higher bid, you are basically forced to guess the best contract. There is very little room to conduct a scientific bidding sequence.

The Opponents Intervene

It would be nice if the opponents always passed. You could tell each other how many points you have, and judge how high to go in the bidding. Sadly, they often overcall at the one- or two-level, and this frequently renders the bid that you wished to make insufficient. Take this hand:

♠ K J 6 3
♡ 8 7
◇ K J 4
♣ 10 8 5 2

Partner opens One Heart, and the next person overcalls Two Clubs. Without the overcall, you would have responded One Spade. Now you are obliged to pass, although there is an explanation in Chapter Ten of a conventional bid which you can make on the hand.

Sometimes the opponents overcall, but the response you would have made is still available. You should generally still make the same bid. There is one proviso here. If the opponents overcall and you bid no-trumps, you promise at least three cards in the suit in which they overcalled, including one of the top three honours. For example, partner opens One Diamond and the next hand overcalls One Spade. You can bid One No-trump on the following hand:

♠ K 10 4
♡ A 5 3
◇ 5 3 2
♣ J 8 5 4

If the king of spades were the king of clubs, however, then bidding One No-trump would be wrong, and you should pass.

One other possibility is that the opponents overcall in a suit or no-trumps and you think that you can defeat the contract that they are in. On this occasion you can double, which tells partner that you have at least nine points and want to defend. If you double a suit contract bid by the opponents you also need a strong holding in their suit. For example, your partner opens One Spade and the next hand overcalls Two Clubs. You would double on the following hand:

♠ 8
♡ A 9 5
◇ Q 4 3 2
♣ A J 10 7 4

If, however, you have agreed to play the convention called the negative double on page 103, you would pass, and partner will bear this in mind and often make a take-out double himself.

Try it Yourself

Exercise 16: Your partner opens One No-trump. What would you respond on the following hand?

♠ K J 8 6 4
♡ 2
♢ K J 8 5 3
♣ K 5

Exercise 17: Your partner opens One Heart. What would you respond on this hand?

♠ 9 6 5 4
♡ 2
♢ 8 6
♣ K Q J 9 6 3

Exercise 18: Your partner opens One Diamond. What would you respond on this hand?

♠ A 4 3 2
♡ 10 9 5 3
♢ 7 5
♣ A 6 2

Exercise 19: Your partner opens Two Spades. What would you respond on this hand?

♠ A 4 3 2
♡ 8 7
♢ K 9 8 7 3
♣ 3 2

Exercise 20: Your partner opens Three Clubs. What would you respond on this hand?

♠ Q 8 6
♡ A 2
♢ Q J 9 6 3
♣ K 5 2

Chapter Five

The Opponents Open

- Overcalling in a Suit
- The One No-trump Overcall
- The Take-Out Double
- Opponents Open One No-trump
- The Jump Overcall
- Game Bids and Other Calls
- Try it Yourself

Overcalling in a Suit

There are three reasons for making an overcall:

a) to attempt to play in a contract yourself

b) to tell partner which is your best suit if you become the defenders

c) to interfere with the opponents' bidding by preventing them from making certain bids

NOTE: All three reasons are important, and you should have one of them whenever making an overcall

What are the minimum requirements for making a one-level overcall? Various books quote differing numbers from a minimum of eight to a minimum of around ten high-card points. We prefer a compromise which we call the Rule of 13, but only for deciding whether to overcall on hands with nine high-card points or fewer. If your high-card points plus the points in the suit total 13 or more, then you should make an overcall. So we recommend that you bid One Spade over One Club on this hand:

♠ A K 10 6 5
♡ 8 4
◇ 8 7 5 3
♣ 9 6

as the hand has seven high-card points, with all seven points in spades, a total of 14. However we would pass this hand:

♠ K 8 7 5 4
♡ A 2
◇ J 9 7 5
♣ 3 2

On hands with ten high-card points and a five-card suit you should generally overcall, but even here we advise having one honour in the five-card suit.

What is the upper limit? This is an area about which experts have different opinions. The consensus seems to be that hands with 18 or more high-card points are too strong to make an overcall at the minimum level, and this is the standard we shall adopt. What do you do on these stronger hands? Well, that depends on how good the suit is, and whether the hand is balanced. We shall look at that shortly.

For now we shall say that the range for an overcall at the lowest level is 10-17 points, but that:

a) You may overcall at the one-level with 7-9 points and a good suit, such that the rule of 13 is followed.

b) There are hands with 15-17 points where you will overcall One No-trump as you shall see shortly.

Can you overcall at the two-level on any hand with ten points? No, again, you need the quality of the suit to be good, and here the requirements are much more stringent, as you are contracting for eight tricks, and the opponents will thus be more likely to double you if you step out of line. To overcall at the two-level on 10 or 11 points you need a six-card suit, and to overcall on 12-14 points you need a very good five-card suit headed by at least two honours. So on this hand you should overcall Two Clubs over any opening bid at the one-level:

♠ A 4
♥ 10 8 4
♦ 6 3
♣ K Q J 5 3 2

However, you should pass on the following hand:

♠ A 4
♥ 10 8 4
♦ Q 3 2
♣ K Q 10 5 3

The One No-trump Overcall

As with an opening bid of One No-trump, the overcall of One No-trump conveys a specific range of points, generally accepted to be 15-17. We use a higher range for the overcall than for the opening bid of One No-trump, as one opponent has already advertised holding at least 12 points, so there are fewer points remaining for your partner. There are one or two other requirements; that the hand is reasonably balanced and that you have at least one high-card, sufficiently guarded, in the opponent's suit. This high-card is called a stopper, and prevents the opponents taking all the tricks in that suit in no-trumps.

This would be a perfect example of a One No-trump overcall after an opposing opening bid of One Heart:

♠ A 5
♡ K 10 8 4
♢ K Q 9 7
♣ K J 3

It is quite acceptable to have a five-card suit for a One No-trump overcall and there will be a few hands that are not balanced on which the bid would also have to be made.

There is a situation when the One No-trump overcall should be made on fewer than 15 points. This is when the opening bid has been followed by two passes and you have the option to pass, ending the auction. This is known as being in the protective position, and One No-trump in such a sequence shows only 11-14 points, very similar to the One No-trump opening bid. For example the following hand would bid One No-trump if the auction went One Heart followed by two passes:

♠ K J 5
♡ Q 10 7 5
♢ A Q 8 4
♣ 10 8

If you have more than 14 points, then you have to make a double which we shall cover shortly. With a balanced hand of 19-21 points, you can bid Two No-trumps if a one-level opening bid is followed by two passes.

The Take-Out Double

We mentioned this very briefly in Chapter Two. Now is the time to cover all the types of hands that will make a double of an opening suit bid:

a) The opponents open the bidding at the one-level (we will consider opening bids at a higher level later). If you do not have a five-card suit, but can support the other three suits, then there is a bid which tells your partner this. It is called the take-out double and says that you have at least 12 points and usually at least three cards in the other three suits, and no more than two of the suit opened. Here is an example of a take-out double of an opening bid of One Club:

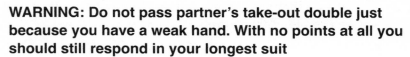

♠ K J 3
♡ Q J 5 2
◇ K Q 10 8
♣ K 8

Partner must choose his or her best suit in response. Only with **at least five and preferably six** of the suit opened should partner pass, attempting to defeat the opponents' contract.

 WARNING: Do not pass partner's take-out double just because you have a weak hand. With no points at all you should still respond in your longest suit

Note that the above hand also fulfils our requirement for an overcall of One No-trump. However, when you have only two of the suit opened, you should prefer the take-out double. If the opponents open in one suit and respond in a different suit, you can still use the take-out double, but now you need at least four cards in each of the two unbid suits, or a very good hand. For example, you are South, and West, the dealer, opens One Club. Partner passes and East responds One Spade. You could now make a take-out double with the following hand:

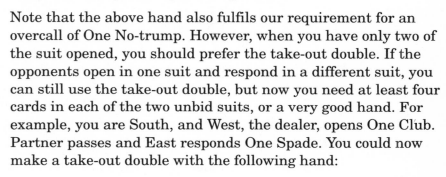

♠ K 7
♡ A Q 10 5
◇ K J 7 3 2
♣ 9 5

Partner will respond to a take-out double by assuming that you have about 13 points. With 0-8, partner bids at the lowest level, with 9-11 partner will jump a level, and with 12 or more partner will bid game or cue-bid the opponent's suit, an artificial bid showing a strong hand and forcing partner to bid. With 7-10 and a balanced hand, partner responds One No-trump. With 11-12 partner will respond Two No-trumps.

b) Any balanced hand with 18 or more points.

♠ A K J 2
♡ Q 10 9
◇ A K 5
♣ K 7 4

The above hand has 20 points and is too strong for an overcall of One No-trump. 'Why not overcall Two No-trumps?,' you may ask. Indeed, the old-fashioned treatment of the Two No-trump overcall was exactly that, the same as a Two No-trump opening bid. Nowadays, however, that usage is rarely adopted (except as we mentioned earlier when an opening bid at the one-level is followed by two passes) and the Two No-trump overcall is another of our special conventions, explained in Chapter Ten.

c) Any hand too strong to make an overcall at the lowest level. Hands with 18 or more high-card points, or any hand that needs little help from partner to make game, should begin with a double. For example:

♠ A K Q 10 7 4
♡ K 2
◇ A K 5 2
♣ 3

If the opponents open at the one-level, then the hand is too strong to overcall One Spade or even Two Spades, which shows a much weaker hand, as we shall see shortly. Including two points for distribution, the hand is worth 21 points. You should double and then bid spades after your partner responds.

d) When the opponents open with a pre-emptive bid, the normal method is to double for take-out asking partner to bid one of the other three suits. Let us say that West, the dealer opens Three Hearts and we have the following hand:

♠ A J 8 4
♡ K 9
◇ A 7 2
♣ K 10 7 5

The best bid is to double. As you are asking partner to bid at a high level, you need a slightly better hand than for a double of a one-level opening bid, around 15 points. Partner will often pass if he thinks you are likely to defeat their contract and not likely to make a contract of your own.

e) If the opponents open at the two-level, showing eight tricks in any suit, then you can still double if you have the other three suits, but you should have four of each and around 15 points.

Opponents Open One No-trump

When the opponents open One No-trump, you can still overcall at the two-level if you have a six-card suit or a very good five-card suit. The following hand would be a sound overcall of Two Spades over the opponent's One No-trump:

♠ K 10 8 7 5 2
♡ A 9
♢ A 6 3
♣ 8 5

However, if the two of spades were the two of clubs then it would be unsound to overcall, and you should pass. An overcall of two of a suit over the the opponent's One No-trump does have an upper limit. With 15 or more points you should start with a double, unless you have a very distributional hand. An example of a correct double of an opening bid of One No-trump:

♠ A K 8
♡ K Q J 7 5
♢ K 4
♣ 8 7 4

This hand is too strong to overcall and should start with a double, showing 15 or more points. The double is a little different from the take-out double of one of a suit. It is essentially a penalty double, but partner will bid if he thinks that is better for you to play the hand.

The Jump Overcall

Opinions differ on how strong a hand you should have to make a jump overcall — in other words to overcall at a level one higher than is necessary. The old-fashioned style was to play that this shows a very strong hand, but such hands can be easily shown by doubling first and then bidding your best suit.

The only system that makes any sense is to play that a jump overcall is either a weak hand or a minimum opening bid, in both cases with a six-card suit. The problem with using the latter is that the hand which makes a simple overcall at the two-level is very similar in terms of high-card points. We shall therefore follow the majority of modern experts and recommend that a jump overcall is an obstructive bid which shows a six-card suit headed by two of the top three honours, and 6-10 high card points. This would be an example of a Two Spade overcall of an opponent's opening bid of One Club:

> ♠ K Q 9 7 5 2
> ♡ 8
> ♢ Q 10 5 3
> ♣ 9 4

When the opponents open One No-trump, their strength is more clearly defined, and the jump overcall must be at the three-level. The normal method is that an overcall of three of a suit over an opponent's One No-trump shows a single-suited hand too strong to make a simple overcall, but with fewer than the 15 high-card points needed to double. For example:

> ♠ A 3
> ♡ Q J 10 9 7 5
> ♢ K Q J 2
> ♣ 7

It is important when you sit down opposite any new partner that, in addition to confirming that you play a weak no-trump (even in Britain many players do not), you agree what strength your jump overcalls show. There is no uniformity of approach.

Game Bids and Other Calls

There are several other bids which can be made when the opponents open the bidding. Overcalling in a game contract should show some expectation of making, but no certainty. Success will depend to a large extent on what partner provides in support. The common feature of all overcalls at the game-level is a long strong suit and fewer than 12 high-card points. On the following hand you would overcall Four Spades:

> ♠ K Q J 10 8 7 5 3
> ♡ 2
> ♢ K 4
> ♣ 10 8

Indeed, you would expect to fail in your contract of Four Spades as often as not, but you are sure that the hand should be played in spades, and therefore go as high as is reasonable.

The other possible bids are the cue-bid of the opponent's suit and the overcall of Two No-trumps. These bids are never played as natural bids by any experts and Chapter Ten discusses a conventional way the bids can be used.

Try it Yourself

Exercise 21: The lady on your right deals and opens One Club. What do you bid on this hand?

♠ 10 9 8 7 4
♡ Q J
♢ K J
♣ Q 5 4 2

Exercise 22: The man on your right opens One Spade. What do you bid on this hand?

♠ K 2
♡ A K 5
♢ Q 9 7 5
♣ K J 10 4

Exercise 23: Partner passes and the next hand opens One No-trump. What do you bid on this hand?

♠ A K J 3
♡ K 10 9 4
♢ K 9 4
♣ Q 7

Exercise 24: The lady on your right opens One Spade. What do you bid on this hand? Yes, it is the same one!

♠ A K J 3
♡ K 10 9 4
♢ K 9 4
♣ Q 7

Exercise 25: Your right-hand opponent opens One Diamond. What do you bid on this hand?

♠ 4
♡ A 2
♢ 8 4 2
♣ Q J 10 9 8 5 3

Chapter Six

The Opener's Rebid

- **When to Pass**
- **Rebidding in No-trumps**
- **Bidding a New Suit**
- **Rebidding Your Suit**
- **Supporting Partner**
- **Jumping a Level**
- **The Reverse**
- **Rebids after One No-trump**
- **Rebids after Two-Level Openings**
- **Rebids after Pre-empting**
- **Try it Yourself**

When a player has opened and received a response, he is in a much better position to judge the combined assets of the partnership. However, while a minimum total high-card points may be easy to ascertain, there may still be virtually no upper limit. Take the following two hands:

♠	A K 8 6	♠	Q J 8 6
♡	K Q 10 5	♡	A J 6
◇	4	◇	A K Q J 5
♣	A K Q 4	♣	J
West		**East**	

West will open One Club, despite having 21 points. Her hand is unsuitable for Two No-trumps, having a singleton. She has no five-card suit, so cannot open with a strong two in a suit, and she does not have enough points to open Two Clubs. East will respond One Diamond. She has enough points to jump to Two Diamonds, but should not do so when she has more than one four-card suit. As can be seen, East-West can take all the tricks, and then some, in a contract of Seven No-trumps!

However, there will be many occasions when the partnership's combined assets are more accurately known, at least to one of the partners. One example is when a player makes one of the limit bids in response, as explained in Chapter Four. The opener needs to select his second bid to tell his partner more about his hand. The number of possible rebids is very similar to the number of opening bids, so that you can see that our tree is spreading its branches very rapidly.

When to Pass

The decision on whether to make a rebid depends on whether partner's response is forcing. The only occasions on which the opener can pass partner's response are:

a) when partner makes a limit bid, either in no-trumps or by raising the opener's suit.

b) when partner makes a bid in a suit other than clubs at the two-level when you have opened One No-trump.

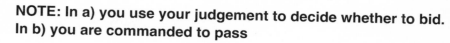

NOTE: In a) you use your judgement to decide whether to bid. In b) you are commanded to pass

Opposite the limit bids you add partner's points to your own, and obtain a range of points for the partnership. If the upper limit is below 25 you always pass. If the lower limit is 25 or more you always bid game. In between you have to make a decision.

For example, you open One Heart on this hand, and partner responds Two Hearts showing 6-9 points:

♠ K J 3
♡ K Q 8 2
♢ A J 6
♣ Q J 5

You deduct one point from this hand for having 4-3-3-3 distribution and it is now 16 points. We would pass if partner responds Two Hearts. The combined points are between 22 and 25 and even with 25 there is no guarantee of making game.

You can also pass whenever partner responds One No-trump or Two No-trumps to your opening bid and you do not have enough points to make game. For example:

♠ K 2
♡ K 7 6 4
♢ A J 9 7
♣ Q 6 5

You open One Diamond and partner responds One No-trump. You should pass. The combined total of points is 19-22 and you have no interest in game. If partner responded Two No-trumps, then we would also pass. The total would then be 23-25. With 23 or 24 you are unlikely to make game, and with 25 not certain.

There is a tendency among most players to overbid. If you are in a contract that is reasonable and you do not think you can make game, then pass.

 TIP: Bid game only when you have 25 points opposite the average number of points for your partner, not his maximum

Rebidding in No-trumps

The opening bid of One No-trump shows a balanced hand with a precise range, 12-14 points. Naturally, when the opener makes a rebid in no-trumps, it also shows a balanced hand, and a precise range. If you open one of a suit and partner responds in a suit at the one-level, then rebidding:

a) One No-trump shows 15-17 points.

b) Two No-trumps shows 18-19 points.

You may notice that we do not list Three No-trumps here. That is because with 20 points and a balanced hand, you would have opened Two No-trumps. The Three No-trump rebid shows a long suit for the opener with a shortage in responder's suit.

If partner responds One No-trump, showing 6-9 points, we similarly raise to Two No-trumps with 15-17 points and to Three No-trumps with 18-19 points.

If partner responds at the two-level, the Two No-trump rebid shows 15-19 points and forces partner to bid again. The reason for this is that partner promised ten points to respond at the two-level. When you have 15 or more points you want to be in game as the combined points are at least 25. Again the Three No-trump rebid is rarely used. Most experts play that it shows 15-19 points with four-card support for responder but, as with many less-common sequences, the average partner would be unsure what the bid meant. On this hand you would open One Heart:

> ♠ A 4 3
> ♡ A Q 9 8 2
> ♢ Q 10 8
> ♣ A 7

If partner responded One Spade you would rebid One No-trump, showing 15-17 points. If partner responded Two Clubs you would bid Two No-trumps showing 15-19 points. Add the queen of clubs to the hand and you would rebid Two No-trumps if partner responded One Spade or Two Clubs.

Old books on bridge taught different ranges for no-trump rebids. British players now usually use the above methods.

Bidding a New Suit

When you have a balanced hand you normally make a rebid in no-trumps. When you have an unbalanced hand you have to do something else. You can still pass if partner makes a limit bid by raising your suit, but if partner makes a limit bid in no-trumps or bids a new suit at the one- or two-level, then you should just bid your second-best suit. It has to be of at least four cards, however. On the following hand you should open One Diamond and rebid Two Clubs if partner responds One Heart, One Spade or even One No-trump.

> ♠ 2
> ♡ A 5
> ◊ K Q 8 6 4 3
> ♣ A J 10 7

You can make a bid of a new suit with quite a good hand — indeed any hand not good enough to jump, which we explain later in this chapter. If the second suit is at the two-level and is a higher-ranking one than the first then you need extra points, as explained in the section on the reverse. You also need extra points if you have to bid your second suit at the three-level. With these provisos you can bid your second suit at the minimum level without any extra points, the same 12 as you promised at the start. You must be careful, however, as partner is not always obliged to bid again. The rule which dictates whether he must bid again is the following one:

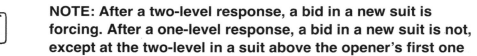

NOTE: After a two-level response, a bid in a new suit is forcing. After a one-level response, a bid in a new suit is not, except at the two-level in a suit above the opener's first one

Also, even though a bid is forcing, it does not necessarily promise any extra points. If partner responds at the two-level, then the combined points are at least 22, and you should continue to describe your hand by bidding your second suit at the lowest level. On the following hand, you would open One Heart and rebid Two Diamonds over a Two Club response:

> ♠ 9 6
> ♡ K Q 10 8 5
> ◊ A 8 7 5
> ♣ K 7

As you shall see later, a rebid of Two Hearts would be non-forcing, but that does not mean you should make that bid in preference to the correct Two Diamonds. Partner should be aware that you may have only 12 points when you rebid Two Diamonds.

We mentioned earlier that bidding a new suit at the three-level shows extra values. Indeed, the following tip is useful (with a few exceptions noted later):

TIP: If you bid a new suit at the three-level, then you are usually saying that the partnership has as at least 25 points and must reach game

Therefore, if you have fewer than 15 points, you will sometimes just have to rebid your suit, and eschew the second suit. For example:

♠ A K 8 7 5
♡ 4
♢ K Q 8 6 2
♣ 10 7

You correctly open One Spade and partner responds Two Hearts. Now you have to rebid Two Spades, as a bid of Three Diamonds would show a better hand. This brings us on to …

Rebidding Your Suit

When you have a minimum hand with a five-card or longer suit, and no other four-card suit, you usually rebid your suit. You may also have to do so when you do not have enough points to bid at a higher level in a new suit, as in our example hand immediately above where you rebid Two Spades.

The rebid of opener's suit shows a minimum hand with 12-15 points and at least a five-card suit. It denies four-card support for partner and is usually not a balanced hand. An example of a hand which would open One Diamond and rebid Two Diamonds after any response up to and including Two Clubs:

♠ K 7
♡ Q 2
♢ A Q J 9 6 4
♣ 10 9 7

Change the ten of clubs to the king of clubs, however, and the hand would be too strong for a rebid of Two Diamonds. It would then be a close choice between a One No-trump rebid or a Three Diamond rebid, which, as you shall see shortly, shows about 15-17 points as well.

The rebid of opener's suit is a non-forcing bid, and partner will usually pass with fewer than 11 points as then a game contract is very unlikely.

Supporting Partner

When you have four cards in partner's suit you should support partner by raising the appropriate number of levels. This depends on the number of points you have. If partner responds one of a major suit, you should raise as follows:

a) to the two-level with 12-15

b) to the three-level with 16-18

c) to game with 19-22

Don't forget that partner will respond to your opening bid with as few as six points, so you should not be too bullish here. You can however, add in shortage points at this stage, if you have four of partner's suit: one for a doubleton, two for a singleton and three for a void. So on this hand you would open One Diamond and raise a One Heart response to Three Hearts:

♠ 10
♡ Q J 8 6
♢ A K 9 7 4
♣ A 8 5

The hand is a minimum for this action, but Two Hearts would be an underbid. Sometimes you will raise partner's major suit with only three-card support, if the alternatives are unattractive. You would do this in preference to rebidding a five-card suit with only one honour, for example. On the following hand you open One Club, and when partner responds One Spade, you should raise to Two Spades:

♠ A 8 4
♡ J
♢ A Q 8 5
♣ J 9 6 4 2

The alternative to raising partner to Two Spades is to rebid Two Clubs. Partner may have no support for clubs, so the latter could be a very poor contract.

If partner responds with two of a minor suit, you are much less likely to raise, as with any reasonably balanced hand you will prefer no-trumps. However, a single raise still shows about 12-15 high-card points. Unbalanced hands with 16 or more points are awkward to handle. For example:

♠ A Q J 7 5
♡ 2
♢ K J 6 4
♣ A Q 4

You open One Spade and partner responds Two Diamonds. You are too strong to raise to Three Diamonds. Four Diamonds is the value bid, but you rarely go to the four-level in a minor suit, as it is higher than the game contract of Three No-trumps. The best alternative is to bid Three Clubs, even though you only have a three-card suit, and hope that partner will bid Three No-trumps. Sometimes there is no perfect bid and you just have to find the best one you can.

Jumping a Level

After the opening bid and response you are often too strong to bid a new suit at the next available level. This is particularly true if partner has responded at the one-level, as a bid of a new suit, as you have seen, will often be non-forcing. The only solution to this problem is to jump a level in a new suit. This is known as a jump shift. Take this hand:

♠ 2
♡ A J 5
♢ K Q 7 6 4
♣ A K J 6

You open One Diamond, and partner responds One Heart. You have 19 points including distribution (one point for a five- and a four-card suit). If you rebid Two Clubs, then that would be non-forcing. You should not support partner's hearts yet. Any double or triple raise of partner's major suit guarantees four-card support, The correct bid is Three Clubs, a jump-shift. This is game-forcing and therefore promises 19 points including distribution, as partner has only promised six points.

However, when you jump in your original suit, you do not promise a hand anywhere near this strength. A jump rebid of opener's first suit shows 15-17 points including distribution, a six-card suit, and is a *non-forcing* bid. An example would be the following hand:

♠ K 2
♡ A K 10 7 5 4
♢ A J 5
♣ 5 4

This hand would open One Heart, and after partner's response of One Spade would rebid Three Hearts. However, if partner has responded at the two-level, then it is normal to play the jump rebid of opener's suit as forcing. This is because partner's two-level response promised ten points. The jump rebid can be made on a wider range of hands, therefore, and shows 15 **or more** points.

There are some single jumps and double jumps in new suits which are normally used as special bids, which are outside the scope of this book.

The Reverse

There is one other rebid that should be mentioned at this stage, as it is often misunderstood by players new to the game. That is the reverse bid. If you start the bidding with one of a suit, and over partner's response

a) bid a new suit at the three-level, or

b) bid a new higher-ranking suit at the two-level

then you have made a reverse bid, and should have at least 16 points including distribution.

An example of a hand on which you can correctly reverse:

♠ K 8
♡ A J 10 5
♢ K Q 8 7 3
♣ A 4

You open One Diamond and partner responds One Spade. You can now bid Two Hearts which is a reverse as you are bidding a higher-ranking suit at the two-level. Your partner can count on you for 16 points. If the ace of clubs were a small club, then you would have to just rebid Two Diamonds, even though you have a four-card heart suit.

NOTE: However, failing to make a reverse bid when you could have does not deny 16 points

If we swap the red suits around on the above hand you would now open One Heart:

> ♠ K 8
> ♡ K Q 8 7 3
> ♢ A J 10 5
> ♣ A 4

If partner responds One Spade, you should rebid Two Diamonds. Even though this is a non-forcing bid, you are not strong enough to jump to Three Diamonds. It would be quite wrong to open One Diamond and reverse with Two Hearts on the next round to show 16 points. **Always** start with the longest suit.

A reverse bid is forcing, but only for one round. The responder is obliged to make another bid, so you could make a reverse on up to 22 points. If you bid a new suit at the three-level that is also a reverse, sometimes called a high reverse, and is forcing to game. On the next hand you would open One Spade, and over a Two Diamond response, bid Three Clubs.

> ♠ A J 10 8 4
> ♡ 6
> ♢ A 6
> ♣ A K J 9 4

All the above sections are concerned with the opener's rebid after he opens one of a suit. We now move on to the opener's rebid after opening One No-trump or higher.

Rebids after One No-trump

When you open One No-trump, you have defined your hand much more accurately than when you open one of a suit. However, partner may not be able to select the final contract immediately; some dialogue may still be required. As you saw in the section on responses, if partner bids Two Clubs, it is the Stayman Convention. You respond to that:

a) Two Diamonds with no major of four cards or more

b) Two Hearts with four or five hearts

c) Two Spades with four or five spades

If you have both four hearts and four spades, you begin with Two Hearts.

If partner raises One No-trump to Two No-trumps, that is simple. With 12 points, you pass, with 14 you bid Three No-trumps. With 13 you have to decide, and features such as a five-card suit and the presence of tens and nines should influence you.

If partner raises One No-trump to Three No-trumps you pass. If he raises to Four No-trumps you bid Six No-trumps or pass depending on the strength of your hand.

The weak take-out should be remembered:

WARNING: If partner bids Two Diamonds, Two Hearts or Two Spades in response to your One No-trump, you MUST pass

When partner jumps to three of any suit in response to your opening bid of One No-trump, you have to bid until you reach game. If you have only two of partner's suit, you bid Three No-trumps. With a minimum hand and three of partner's suit you raise partner. With a maximum hand and three or four of partner's suit, you can bid another suit in which you hold the ace. This is called a cue-bid, and will be explained in more detail in Chapter Ten.

Rebids after Two-Level Openings

When you open at the two-level you are showing a strong hand, and if partner responds, you generally continue to describe your hand. After you open Two Diamonds, Two Hearts or Two Spades, if partner bids anything other than Two No-trumps you must continue until you reach game, bidding your second suit or rebidding your first suit as appropriate. If partner bids Two No-trumps, the negative response, you can still bid a second suit. Partner must bid again, but if you rebid your original suit, partner can pass.

When you open Two Clubs, if partner bids anything other than Two Diamonds you must continue until you reach game. If partner responds Two Diamonds, your rebids are as follows:

a) Two Hearts, Two Spades, Three Clubs or Three Diamonds. This shows a good suit, and is forcing to game.

> ♠ A 8
> ♡ A K J 10 5 4 2
> ◇ A K 7
> ♣ A

On this hand you rebid Two Hearts. There is no need to jump to Three Hearts or Four Hearts. Partner is obliged to bid again and you may still be able to make a slam.

b) Two No-trumps: 23-24 balanced

NOTE: This is the only rebid after a Two Club opening bid which partner can pass!

c) Three No-trumps: 25-27 balanced

d) Four No-trumps 28-30 balanced

Over the above, a new suit by the responder is natural and forcing, except that, after the Two No-trump rebid, Three Clubs is again the Stayman Convention.

When you open Two No-trumps partner is not obliged to bid, but when he does, you must continue until game is reached. If partner bids Three Clubs, it is again the Stayman Convention, and you respond in the same way as after opening One No-trump, except at a higher level.

If partner responds Three Diamonds, Three Hearts, Three Spades or Four Clubs, he is making a natural bid and you must bid again, either supporting partner, going back to Three No-trumps (if possible) or bidding another suit in which you hold the ace (a cue-bid).

Rebids after Pre-empting

When you open at the three-level or above, you are making a pre-emptive bid. You don't intend at the time to make a rebid. As far as you are concerned you have had your say and the main purpose was to jam the communication channels of the opponents. However, partner is sometimes the one with the good hand. If partner bids any game, you should pass. If partner bids a new suit which is not game then you should bid any suit in which you hold a singleton or top honour card.

Try it Yourself

Exercise 26: You open One Heart on this hand, and partner responds One No-trump. What do you do next?

♠ A K 7
♥ J 9 7 5 3
♦ K Q 6
♣ A 5

Exercise 27: You open One Spade and partner responds Two Diamonds. What do you bid on this hand?

♠ Q J 8 6 5
♥ A 5
♦ K J 10 6
♣ J 5

Exercise 28: You open One Heart and partner bids One Spade. What do you bid next?

♠ Q 8 6 5
♥ A K 10 6 5 2
♦ K 3
♣ 2

Exercise 29: You open One Club and partner bids One Spade. What do you bid next?

♠ K 4
♥ A 8
♦ K 5 3
♣ A K J 10 8 6

Exercise 30: You open One Diamond and partner responds Two Clubs. What do you bid?

♠ Q
♥ K Q J 5
♦ A Q J 6 4
♣ A 9 4

Chapter Seven

Continuing the Auction

■ **Responding to Overcalls**

■ **Giving Preference**

■ **Selecting the Final Contract**

■ **Fourth-Suit Forcing**

■ **Forcing or Non-Forcing?**

■ **Slam Bidding**

■ **Try it Yourself**

We have laid the groundwork for good bidding in our previous chapters on the opening bids, responses, overcalls and rebids. However, the auction does not always end there. Quite often there are more than three bids made by a partnership, and the author can recall a very experienced English International pair having an auction against him lasting 26 bids in total. You will find, however, that after three bids you will have a good idea of the combined assets of the partnership. In this chapter we will look at ways of continuing the auction where necessary and a few conventional aids that you can employ.

Responding to Overcalls

When partner overcalls, you can assume only that he has ten points, and don't forget that he may have a little less than this. As partner ought to have a five-card suit, to support partner you now need only three cards in that suit and 6-9 points. With 10-12 points you can jump to the three-level. Although partner may have only ten points, at least you have good support for him. When you have two or fewer cards in partner's suit and a balanced hand you can respond One No-trump with 8-11 points and Two No-trumps with 12-14 points. Note that the requirements here have been increased from those for responding to an opening bid. Hands other than the above can either bid a new suit at the next available level, or if you have enough points to insist on game, you can bid the suit which the opponents opened. On the following hand, if partner bids One Spade over One Heart, you can cue-bid Two Hearts:

♠ K 2
♡ J 5 3
♢ A K 9 8
♣ A J 6 4

To respond Two Clubs or Two Diamonds would not force partner to bid again, whereas the bid of the opponent's suit tells him that you have enough points for game, but you do not yet know which game you should be playing.

Giving Preference

When partner has bid two suits you should assume that the first one is longer than the second, although there will be occasions when they are of equal length. Unless you know that you have 25 points between the two hands, you should tell partner which suit you prefer, or whether you want to play in no-trumps. Take the following hand:

♠ Q J 9 8 5
♥ A 3 2
♦ 10 5
♣ 8 6 2

Partner opens One Heart and you respond One Spade. Now partner rebids Two Clubs. Partner must have at least five hearts and at least four clubs. You should bid Two Hearts.

False Preference

Interestingly, if the two of hearts in the above hand were the two of diamonds, you would still bid Two Hearts over partner's rebid of Two Clubs. Even though you prefer clubs to hearts, if partner does have only seven cards in total in each suit, he will be better off with five in one hand and two in the other.

The choice of Two Hearts is sometimes called false preference, and one of its advantages is that partner can bid again with a good hand.

TIP: A 5-2 combined holding usually plays better than a 4-3

In the majority of cases, partner will pass when you give preference. He will need quite a bit of extra strength to press on, so you should not make the bid when you have enough for game, nor even when you are close to that goal:

♠ Q J 9 8 5
♥ A 3
♦ A 10 5
♣ 8 6 2

For example, on this hand you should respond One Spade to One Heart, as before, but over partner's rebid of Two Clubs you should continue with Two No-trumps. This shows exactly the same number of points as an initial response of Two No-trumps, namely 10-12.

Selecting the Final Contract

When you know roughly how many points you have between the partnership you are much better placed to select the final contract. You will see shortly how you can get partner to bid again when you do not yet know the correct contract. There are three scenarios where you can select the contract:

a) You know you do not have enough points for game.

b) You know you have enough points for game, but not enough for slam.

c) You know you have enough points for slam.

When you do not know which of a), b) or c) applies, then you need to continue to describe your hand, either by giving preference for one of partner's suits, rebidding your suit, or bidding no-trumps as appropriate. You shall also look shortly at ways of ensuring partner bids again.

a) When you know you do not have enough points for game, you should endeavour to end the bidding as soon as possible. Let us say that you have this hand:

♠ A 7 5 4
♡ K Q 7 5 3 2
♢ 4
♣ 6 4

Partner opens One Diamond and you respond One Heart. You are disappointed to hear partner rebid Two Diamonds. You should not bid Two Spades now. As you shall see shortly this is forcing. You should bid Two Hearts, a non-forcing bid which partner will always pass.

b) When you know you have enough points for game, you usually just bid it! Take this hand:

♠ K 5
♡ Q 8
♢ A Q 8 6 4 2
♣ K 9 4

Partner opens One No-trump and it is tempting to bid the excellent diamond suit. However you know the hand belongs in game, but slam is very unlikely. On February 29th, Five Diamonds might be better than Three No-trumps. Today you should just bid Three No-trumps.

c) When you know you have enough points for slam you can often just bid it. If someone criticises your unsophisticated approach, ignore them as you notch up 12 tricks:

♠ A
♡ A K Q 8 5 4
♢ A 10 6 4
♣ 6 4

This hand has 19 points including distribution. If partner opened One No-trump, we would respond Six Hearts. It is true, the opponents may have the ace and king of clubs between them. However, only if the opening leader has both will you necessarily be defeated.

Fourth-Suit Forcing

One gadget which is very useful in bidding is called fourth-suit forcing. Let us see two examples of it in use:

♠ A K Q 8 6 4	♠ 7 2
♡ K 10 6 4	♡ A J 3
♢ 10	♢ Q 5
♣ J 9	♣ K Q 10 8 3 2
West	**East**

West opens One Spade and East responds Two Clubs, showing at least ten points. Now West can bid Two Hearts, her second suit, which is better than bidding Two Spades, as her partner may still have four hearts. East knows that the partnership has enough points for game, but is unsure in which suit. She should bid Three Diamonds, the fourth suit, which says nothing about her holding in diamonds, but asks her partner which game she thinks is best. West should rebid Three Spades, to show the six-card suit, because she has a poor holding in diamonds. East can then go on to Four Spades, which is a much better contract than Three No-trumps.

Another example:

♠ Q 9 8 4	♠ J 10 3
♡ K	♡ A Q 7 5 4
♢ A Q 5 4 2	♢ K J 3
♣ A 10 3	♣ Q 5
West	**East**

Here West will open One Diamond and over her partner's bid of One Heart, she should bid One Spade, because her hand is not quite balanced enough for One No-trump, and her partner may also have four spades. East should now bid Two Clubs, the fourth suit, saying that she has enough points for game, and West should now bid Three No-trumps, because she has a stopper in clubs.

Fourth-suit forcing is very useful but only when you cannot make an alternative bid. If you have a natural bid you should make it. Take the next example:

West	East
♠ A 9	♠ 8 4
♡ Q 2	♡ A J 10 9 5 4
◇ K Q 8 6 5	◇ 10 7
♣ K 6 4 2	♣ A J 3
West	**East**

West opens One Diamond and East responds One Heart. Now West should rebid Two Clubs and East can bid a natural, but non-forcing, Three Hearts, saying that she has six hearts and nearly enough for game. We would now bid Four Hearts on the West hand because the queen of hearts is likely to be a very useful card when partner has bid the suit twice. East should not use the fourth-suit bid of Two Spades on this hand, because she has a more descriptive bid available. Change the jack of hearts to the king of hearts, and she should use the fourth-suit bid of Two Spades. The problem is that Three Hearts is non-forcing and she then has enough points to want to be in game.

The general rules for fourth-suit forcing are often not agreed by top players. For this book we shall adopt the simple principle that a bid of the fourth-suit says that you have 25 points between the two hands, and should keep the bidding open until you reach game. If you form a regular partnership in bridge, then you can discuss with your partner how and when to vary from this blanket rule.

Forcing or Non-Forcing?

There are many other situations, other than when the fourth suit has been bid, which are forcing and partner is obliged to bid again. The weakness of the early bridge computers was in recognising these, and often they dropped an auction just as it was getting going! There are a number of useful rules which tell the beginner which bids are forcing and which are not.

Forcing bids

a) any change of suit by responder after one of a suit is opened

b) any rebid in a new suit by opener after a two-level response

c) any rebid by opener at the two-level in a higher suit than the first

d) any jump by opener, other than a jump rebid in the opener's suit or a jump raise of partner's suit after a one-level response

e) any jump by responder, other than a jump rebid in the responder's suit, or a jump raise of one of opener's suits

f) any new suit at the three-level, **with the exception of k) below**, is forcing. If a suit has been bid and raised, then it is called a game try and invites partner to bid game in the first suit. Otherwise it is a natural bid and is forcing to game

g) the bid of the fourth suit is forcing until game is reached

h) a two-level opening, **with the exception of l) and m) below**, is forcing to game

Non-forcing bids

i) any limit bid in no-trumps as described in Chapter Four

j) any raise of opener's suit is a limit raise and non-forcing

k) a new suit at the three-level is non-forcing by a player who responded One No-trump on the previous round. It shows a six- or seven-card suit and 6-9 points

l) the rebid Two No-trumps after an opening Two Clubs and a negative Two Diamond response

m) the rebid of opener's suit after any other two-level opening and a Two No-trump negative reply

n) any rebid of opener's suit or responder's suit, or any preference to one of opener's suits or one of responder' suits is non-forcing, unless either f) or g) applies

o) any bid of a game or slam contract by opener or responder

The above is a good generalisation of a complicated area of bridge. Do not worry if it is a lot to take in all at once. Many players who have playing for years are unsure whether bids are forcing or not. If you are unsure whether a bid is forcing or not, then fall back on the following tip:

TIP: 'When in doubt, bid what you think you can make', is a good motto

Slam Bidding

There are a couple of approaches one can adopt when bidding a slam, including another convention which all beginners will need to know:

Blackwood

The **Blackwood Convention** is a method of ascertaining how many aces partner has. Let us say that you have the following hand:

♠ A 4
♡ K 8 6
◇ K Q 9 4
♣ K Q 3 2

Partner opens One Heart, you bid Two Clubs, and partner rebids Three Hearts. This is a forcing bid, as we saw earlier, promising at least 15 points and a six-card suit. It looks like you have a slam on the cards, as you have 17 points, and can add one for the doubleton making 18. Before you bid a slam, you can use the Blackwood Convention which asks partner how many aces he has.The responses are as follow:

Five Clubs	No aces (or four aces)
Five Diamonds	One ace
Five Hearts	Two aces
Five Spades	Three aces

Partner will have at least one ace to make up his 15 points. If he responds Five Diamonds, you will be very disappointed, but will then bid Five Hearts, a bid which commands partner to pass. If he responds Five Hearts, showing two aces, you will raise to Six Hearts. Finally, if he bids Five Spades, showing all three aces, you will bid Seven Hearts. Two possible hands for partner are as follows:

♠ K Q J 2
♡ A Q J 10 9 7 5
◇ 4
♣ 9

This is a perfectly sound rebid of Three Hearts by partner, with the excellent distribution, but there are two aces missing.

♠ 4 2
♡ A Q J 8 5 2
◇ A 9 6
♣ A 8

Again a standard Three Heart rebid, with 15 points, and now you have 13 tricks in hearts or no-trumps.

On occasion, if and only if you discover that you have all four aces between the two hands, you may want to ask for kings. This is done with a bid of Five No-trumps after the response to the Blackwood Four No-trumps has been made. The responses to indicate how many kings are held are similar:

Six Clubs	No kings (or four kings)
Six Diamonds	One king
Six Hearts	Two kings
Six Spades	Three kings

BEWARE: Use the Blackwood Five No-trump asking bid only when you are interested in grand slam

When you bid Five No-trumps you guarantee that you have all four aces. Partner is therefore quite within his rights to jump to seven if he thinks he can make it (for example when he has a long suit). Also make sure that whatever response partner may make will not be at too high a level, otherwise you may go past the last making contract. In this regard you should take particular care when the suit you intend to play in is either clubs or diamonds.

Cue-Bids

The Blackwood convention is one of the most overused gadgets in bridge. It should be used only when you have the values for a slam, and the only question you need answered is how many aces the opponents have. It should not normally be used on any hand which has a void, and on other occasions a method of moving towards a slam called cue-bidding may be more appropriate. This is particularly the case when you are missing the ace and king of one suit, and want partner to cue-bid before bidding a slam. The following hand shows both these points well:

♠ K 10 6	♠ A Q J 9 8 5
♡ A Q 8 4	♡ K 6 2
◇ 10 9 6	◇ None
♣ K 4 2	♣ A 8 5 3
West	**East**

West opens One No-trump, showing 12-14 points and East should not immediately bid Four Spades, but should bid Three Spades, showing the values for game and a good five-card suit. Including distribution, East has 16 points, and, if her partner has spade support, she will be able to add points for the void. West will raise to Four Spades with only 12 points but now East should bid Five Clubs, a cue-bid, showing the ace of clubs. West will bid Five Hearts showing the ace of hearts and East should take a chance with Six Spades. If her partner had cue-bid Five Diamonds, however, then East should sign off with Five Spades. Partner's diamond control would then duplicate the one held by East and not be as useful. The correct method of playing the hand is shown on page 86. The contract is an excellent one and should make easily.

There are two styles for cue-bids. The so-called Italian style, preferred by the author, is that when you cue-bid you have one of the ace, king, void or singleton of the suit you cue-bid. Another style is to cue-bid the ace or a void and not to cue-bid a singleton or the king in the first instance. In the latter style you usually cue-bid any kings at the five-level. Cue-bids should not be confused with natural suit bids.

NOTE: The normal rule is that after you have bid and supported a suit, a new suit at the three-level is natural and forcing, and invites partner to bid game in the first suit. A new suit at the four-level or above is a cue-bid showing the first or second-round control as agreed by the partnership

In the following sequence, the last bid in each case is a cue-bid:

a) One Heart—Three Hearts—Four Clubs

b) One Club—One Spade—Three Spades—Four Diamonds

c) One Spade—Four Spades—Five Diamonds

It should be noted that you need to have interest in a slam to cue-bid, hence a non-minimum hand. Partner is perfectly entitled to jump to a slam immediately with the right hand.

Try it Yourself

Exercise 31: Over One Heart on your left, partner overcalls One Spade and the next hand passes. What do you bid?

♠ K 8
♡ A K 10 2
◇ K 9 7 3
♣ 10 9 5

Exercise 32: Your partner opens One Heart. You respond One Spade, and partner rebids Two Diamonds. What next?

♠ J 8 7 6
♡ 7 5
◇ 4 2
♣ K Q 9 8 7

Exercise 33: You respond to One Heart with One Spade and partner rebids Two Clubs. What do you bid?

♠ A Q 8 7 5
♡ K 7
◇ Q 7
♣ K 8 6 4

Exercise 34: You open One Spade and partner raises to Three Spades. What do you do next?

♠ A K J 9 8 6
♡ A K J 4
◇ J 7 4
♣ None

Exercise 35: Partner opens One Heart and you respond Two Clubs. Now partner bids Two Diamonds. Over to you!

♠ A K 3
♡ 4
◇ K J 8 6
♣ A K 7 6 4

Chapter Eight

Declarer Play

- **The Finesse**
- **The Cross-Ruff**
- **The Hold-Up**
- **Ruffing Losers**
- **Keeping the Danger Hand off Lead**
- **Disposing of Losers**
- **Card Combinations**
- **Percentages**
- **Try it Yourself**

We are now going to look as some common card-play techniques which will enable you to make more tricks in the contracts you will now bid so well!

The Finesse

As we explained in Chapter One, when you play the hand you are trying to make as many tricks as you called in the bidding. The opponents are trying to prevent you from doing this. How do you set about the play of the hand? Let us see:

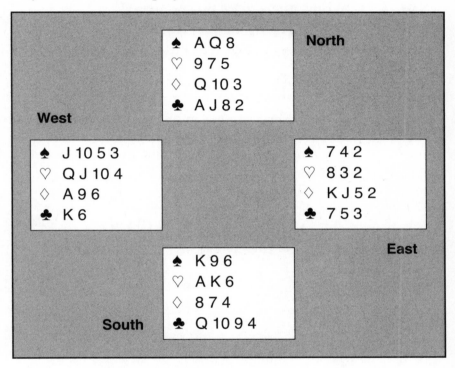

On the above hand, South is dealer and he opens One No-trump. North responds Three No-trumps. He knows that between the two hands there are 25 points and this should be enough to make a game contract. West leads the queen of hearts. How should South plan to make nine tricks?

Well, the first rule is to count how many tricks you are certain to make. In spades you must make three tricks, the ace, king and queen. In hearts you have two sure tricks. The only other certain trick you can make without losing the lead is the ace of clubs. So your total of certain tricks is six. How do you plan to make three more? A good rule is to start on your longest suit, in this case clubs. You are missing the king and the correct way to play is to win the first trick with the ace of hearts and then to lead the queen of clubs. If West plays a small card, you also play small from dummy. This is known as a finesse. You eventually make four club tricks, as the king will be captured on the second round. You thus make nine tricks by way of three spades, two hearts and four clubs. The lessons from this hand:

TIP: Follow these four steps when you play any hand:

a) Count how many tricks you are certain to make

b) How many extra do you need?

c) Which is my longest suit?

d) How can I make extra tricks in that suit?

The Cross-Ruff

Usually when you are in a trump contract it is correct to start by drawing the opponents' trumps. However, when you have singletons or voids in both hands, it is often wrong. Take the following hand:

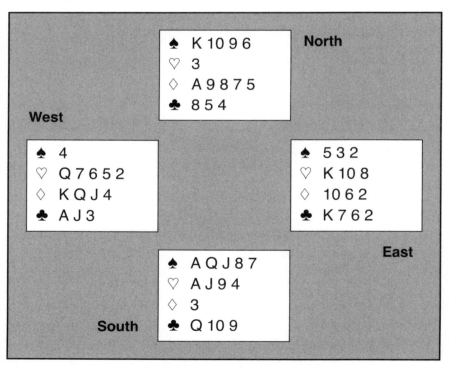

South is the dealer and opens One Spade, and North raises to Three Spades. This is a good example of adding on extra points because you have a singleton, and also for having a five-card suit and a four-card suit. So the North hand is worth ten points. South now continues with Four Spades. West leads the king of diamonds, as she has a sequence headed by the king. How should South play? Again, you count your certain tricks and you have five trumps and two aces, clearly not enough. The right way to proceed is not to draw trumps but to play a cross-ruff. You should win the ace of diamonds and then ruff a diamond. Then play the ace of hearts and ruff a heart. You continue with another diamond ruff, another heart ruff, a further diamond ruff and then ruff your last heart. Then you ruff your last diamond with a high spade and still have one high trump to come. Ten tricks instead of seven!

The Hold-Up

This sounds like a play that you might find in an American bar in the Mid-West, but in reality it is a means of stopping the opponents from running a long suit. An example:

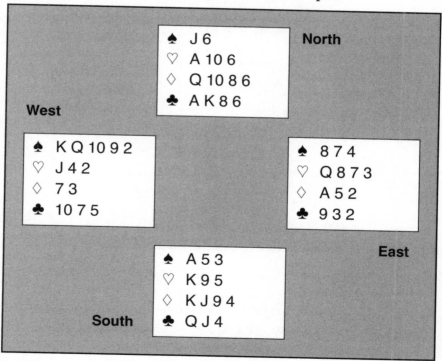

```
                         ♠ J 6            North
                         ♡ A 10 6
                         ♢ Q 10 8 6
                         ♣ A K 8 6
West

      ♠ K Q 10 9 2                    ♠ 8 7 4
      ♡ J 4 2                         ♡ Q 8 7 3
      ♢ 7 3                           ♢ A 5 2
      ♣ 10 7 5                        ♣ 9 3 2
                                                  East

                         ♠ A 5 3
                         ♡ K 9 5
                         ♢ K J 9 4
              South      ♣ Q J 4
```

South is dealer and opens One No-trump, showing a balanced hand with 12-14 points. North raises to Three No-trumps. He knows that the combined hands have at least 26 points. Unfortunately West leads the king of spades, attacking your weak suit. Now you should 'hold-up' the ace of spades instead of winning the first trick. If the opponents continue with the queen of spades, you should hold-up again. You win the third trick and then lead the king of diamonds. East wins this trick with the ace of diamonds but she is now out of spades and the defence cannot then cash their remaining spade winners.

Ruffing Losers

This is is the hand (rotated for convenience) which, on page 80, North-South bid to the excellent contract of Six Spades.

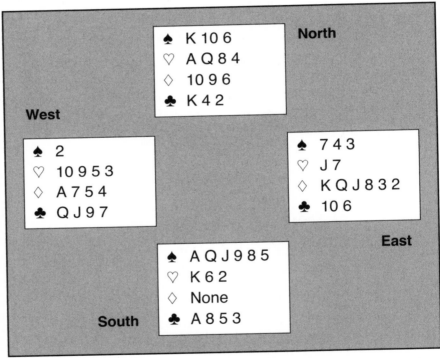

West leads the queen of clubs, but declarer wins with the king and leads a club to the ace. It is important that he does not draw trumps just yet, as he needs a trump in North to dispose of his club loser. Instead, he plays a third club, which West wins. She tries to cash the ace of diamonds, more in hope than expectation. South trumps this and then trumps his losing club with the king of spades, while East has to discard. South has thus created an extra trick by ruffing a loser in the hand with the fewer trumps. Only now does he draw trumps, having disposed of his club loser. He therefore makes twelve tricks — six spades, three hearts, two clubs and one club ruff in the North hand.

Keeping the Danger Hand off Lead

Another important theme in bridge is to play the hand in such a way that when you lose a trick you do so to an opponent who cannot do you any harm. The following hand is a good example:

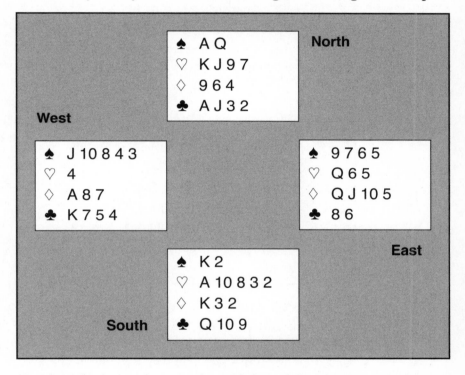

North is dealer and opens One Club and South responds One Heart. North now raises to Two Hearts and South correctly bids Four Hearts because he has 13 points, including one for the doubleton. West leads the jack of spades. Now the declarer should play the queen of spades and then lead the king of hearts and then the jack of hearts. If East plays a small heart, the declarer should run the jack, playing a low card from the South hand. If West were to win with the queen of hearts, then the opponents would not be able to lead diamonds without allowing the king to win a trick. If West has the king of clubs or if East has the ace of diamonds or queen of hearts, South will succeed in his contract — he would be very unlucky to go down, but would have given it his best shot.

Disposing of Losers

The next hand is similar but involves a different approach:

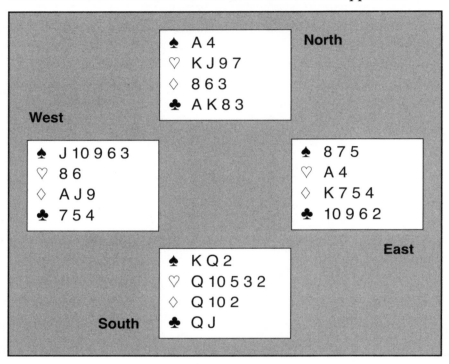

North is dealer and opens One Club, the lower of two four-card suits, and South responds One Heart. North again raises to Two Hearts and South continues Four Hearts. West leads the jack of spades and the declarer wins with the ace. Now if South plays a trump, the defence should win and can take three diamond tricks. Indeed they should, as East should switch to diamonds, dummy's weak suit. Therefore declarer should first play the king and queen of spades, discarding a diamond from the North hand, and only then play a trump. Now the defenders can win only two diamond tricks and the ace of trumps. It should be noted that the opening lead of the nine of diamonds would have defeated the game, as the defence could then take three diamonds and a heart. No doubt East will be quick to berate his partner for not finding it, but bridge players are notorious for being result merchants!

Card Combinations

The following card combinations are some of the most common. We shall not go into the percentages for each, but merely give the correct play of the suit, assuming you want to make as many tricks as possible. 'x' is used to denote a card below a ten.

a) AQJxxx opposite xxxxx: lay down the ace

b) AQJxx opposite xxxxx: play towards the queen and finesse

c) AKJxx opposite xxxx: lead the ace and then the king (all other things being equal)

d) AKJxx opposite xxx: lead the ace and then towards the jack and finesse

The last two combinations give rise to the little bridge tip:

TIP: 'Eight ever, nine never'

This means that with eight cards between the two hands missing the queen, you always finesse, with nine cards you never do. In reality there will be reasons to break this rule on many occasions.

e) AKQ10 opposite xxx: lead the ace, king and then queen

f) AKQ10x opposite x: lead towards the ten and finesse

g) AJ10xx opposite xxxx: finesse the ten first and then the jack afterward. This is known as a double finesse

h) AQ10xx opposite xxxx: finesse the ten and then the queen. This can vary if you need five tricks to make the contract when you should finesse the queen

i) AK10x opposite Q9xxx. Start with the ace. If either opponent shows out, you can then finesse the other hand for the jack

j) KQ10xx opposite xxx. Play low to the king, but whether or not it wins play low to the ten on the second round.

Percentages

Contrary to popular belief, maths does not play a major part in bridge, but it is useful to know the chances of a suit dividing between the opponents in the various ways. When the opponents have two, four or six cards between them, those cards are more likely to be unevenly divided. When they have three or five cards between them, then a a 2-1 or 3-2 distribution is a big favourite. All figures are to the nearest percentage.

Probability of Each Division of a Suit

Opponents have two cards

West	East	%
2	0	26%
1	1	48%
0	2	26%

Opponents have three cards

West	East	%
3	0	11%
2	1	39%
1	2	39%
0	3	11%

Opponents have four cards

West	East	%
4	0	5%
3	1	25%
2	2	41%
1	3	25%
0	4	5%

Opponents have five cards

West	East	%
5	0	2%
4	1	14%
3	2	34%
2	3	34%
1	4	14%
0	5	2%

Opponents have six cards

West	East	%
6	0	1%
5	1	7%
4	2	24%
3	3	36%
2	4	24%
1	5	7%
0	6	1%

Try it Yourself

Exercise 36: West plays Three No-trumps on the lead of the four of spades to South's jack. Plan the play?

West	East
♠ K Q 8	♠ 7 5 2
♡ A Q 3	♡ K 7 5
◇ J 10 8 6	◇ A Q 9 7
♣ A 5 4	♣ K 8 3

West   **East**

Exercise 37: West is in Four Hearts on the lead of the king of clubs from North. How would you play?

West	East
♠ A 4	♠ K Q 6 3
♡ A Q 8 6 5	♡ K J 2
◇ K 6 4	◇ 8 7 5 2
♣ A 9 7	♣ 8 6

West   **East**

Exercise 38: You are in Five Diamonds, by West, and North leads the queen of clubs. What is your line?

West	East
♠ 6	♠ A Q 8
♡ A K 4	♡ Q 8 5
◇ K Q J 9 8 4	◇ 10 7 6 3
♣ A 7 4	♣ 9 8 5

West   **East**

Exercise 39: You are in Three No-trumps as West on the lead of the queen of spades. You win the lead; what next?

West	East
♠ A K	♠ 7 5
♡ K Q 4	♡ J 8
◇ A 10 8 6 3	◇ K Q J 2
♣ Q 9 3	♣ K 10 5 4 2

West   **East**

Chapter Nine

Defence

- **Basic Principles**
- **The Opening Lead**
- **The Rule of Eleven**
- **Signalling**
- **Giving Count**
- **Counting Declarer's Points**
- **Try it Yourself**

Basic Principles

Defence is a difficult area of the game. The two defenders can each see 26 cards, but unlike the declarer, they are unaware of the combined assets of their side. As we stated earlier, the main object is to prevent the declarer from making his or her contract. Defence is like solving a jigsaw puzzle. The two players are slowly putting together the complete picture, and gleaning information from plays that both do and do not occur. Towards the end of the hand, each defender can draw certain conclusions about declarer's holding, but the first thing to mention is that it is essential to remember what has gone, particularly the high cards in each suit. A bridge proverb recommends that you:

TIP: Keep track of the ace, king, queen, jack

Furthermore it is often necessary to keep a count of each suit as well. You can usually work out which suits partner or declarer has left by counting and observation. You may find this difficult at first, but with practice it becomes easy. The blackjack professional has no difficulty in counting six decks of cards dealt two cards per second!

The tools that the defenders have at their disposal are summarised in this chapter. These include the information for the opening lead and the order in which small cards are played, known as signalling. It should be stressed here that the play of the cards is the only acceptable signalling method, and any other gesture, mannerism or remark is quite out of order and a breach of the Laws of Bridge.

The Opening Lead

The opening lead is the defence's first salvo. It is important that it is carefully chosen, and that partner will know the possible holdings you have in the suit led.

You usually choose your longest and strongest suit to lead, particularly in no-trumps, and also, with some exceptions, in trump contracts. There are two types of opening lead, honour leads and small card leads. Included in the latter is the traditional 'fourth best' which most beginners are taught. There are many books on opening leads, advocating fancy methods. In this book we will stick with the tried and tested systems. In each example 'x' agains stands for a card below the 10. Adding or removing small cards does not change the lead.

Top of a Sequence Leads
From the following holdings, always lead the top card:
AK, AKQ, AKJ, AKxx, KQJ, KQ10, KQ9, QJ10, QJ9, J109, J108, 109xx, whether the contract is in no-trumps or in a suit.

Fourth Best Leads
From the following holdings always lead the fourth best:
KJxx, K10xx, Kxxx, Qxxx, Jxxx. From **Axxx, AQxx** or **AJxx**, lead the fourth-best in no-trumps, but do not lead the suit against a trump contract.

From the following holdings, lead the fourth best in no-trumps, the top card against a suit contract:
KQxx, QJxx, J10xx.

Interior Sequence Leads
From the following lead the second card:
KJ10x, Q109x, K109x, AJ10x. In the last of these do not lead the suit at all against a trump contract

Leads from Weak Suits
From a doubleton, lead the higher card in all cases. This is true for **Ax, Kx, Qx, Jx, 10x** or **xx**. You would not usually lead a doubleton honour unless partner had bid the suit. From **xxx**, opinions vary, and you should ask your partner what she leads from this holding. Many top pairs lead the middle card, and then follow on the next round with the higher, the so-called MUD convention, standing for Middle-Up-Down. From **xxxx** or **xxxxx** the recommended lead is again the second-highest card.

Exceptions

WARNING: Generally avoid leading a low card from a suit in which you have the ace against a suit contract. For each time it is right there will be two times it costs

If you have to lead the suit, then lead the ace. If you have to lead a three-card suit headed by an honour, then lead the third card; partner may be misled, but sometimes this cannot be avoided.

Trump Leads
Beginners often lead trumps, 'the only safe lead I had, partner,'

but in general trump leads are to be avoided. The most common reasons to lead a trump are as follows:

a) The dummy has given a preference to one of the two suits bid by declarer.

b) The opponents have bid on over your game contract as a sacrifice, and you want to stop them conducting a cross-ruff.

c) Your partner has passed a take-out double at the one- or two-level, attempting to achieve a penalty.

The Rule of Eleven

Why do you lead the fourth-best card of your longest suit? This convention allows partner to judge which card to play and to work out which cards declarer may have. Here is an example:

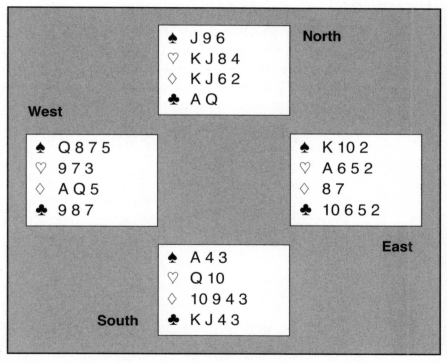

North opens One Diamond, and South responds Two No-trumps, showing 10-12 points and a balanced hand. North correctly raises to Three No-trumps. West leads the five of spades, the fourth best of her longest suit. The declarer plays low from dummy and now East has to make a decision. One general guideline is that second hand plays low and third hand plays high, but this is only a rough-and-ready rule. A better method for East to follow is to deduct the value of the card led from 11 and this gives the number of cards which the three other players have higher than the card led. In this case the answer is six; East can see five of these (the six, nine and jack in dummy and the ten and king in his own hand). He therefore knows that South has only one card higher than the five, so he should play the ten and not the king. If South's high card is the ace, playing the king will allow the declarer to make two spade tricks. The defence will now always take three spade tricks and two red aces. Sometimes it is not possible to tell which card declarer has higher than the one led, but North can also follow the principle of playing the card immediately below dummy's highest card, in this case the ten.

Signalling

It is a breach of the laws of the game to make any signal to your partner other than with cards, so what do we mean by signalling? It is a means of telling partner that you like her lead and want the suit continued. The way it works that if you play a high card on partner's lead you are encouraging; if you

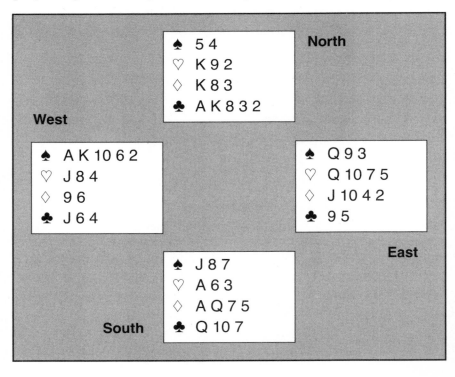

play a low card you are discouraging. Similarly if you discard a high card in a suit, you want it led; if you discard a low card you don't want it led. The diagram at the bottom of the previous page is an example.

South opens One No-trump and North raises to Three No-trumps. West leads the ace of spades. Now East should play the nine, a high card, showing that she likes the spade lead. West can then continue with a small spade to the queen, and East will return a spade allowing the defence to take the first five spade tricks. Note that if West plays the king of spades on the second trick, then the defence can only take three spade tricks and the declarer will make two hearts, three diamonds and five clubs for a total of ten tricks instead of eight!

Change the hand slightly and we have a different situation:

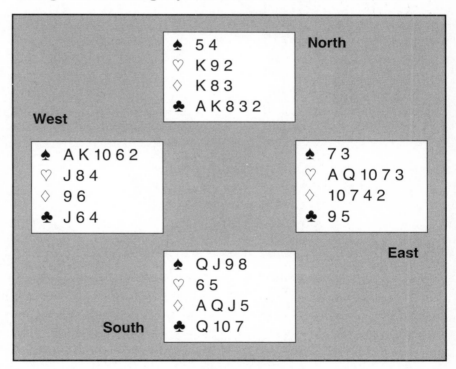

Now when West leads the ace of spades after the same auction (One No-trump—Three No-trumps), East should play the three of spades, her lowest card, to say that she doesn't want spades continued. If West now leads the jack of hearts the contract is defeated, but if West leads a small spade (or either minor suit) the declarer makes the contract.

Giving Count

Another very popular method of signalling is to give count when you follow suit with small cards. The traditional method of doing this is to play as high a card as you can afford when you have an even number of cards in the suit led and the lowest card you have in the suit when you have an odd number of cards. This is a common method of signalling on declarer's lead, and often on partner's lead. Take this hand:

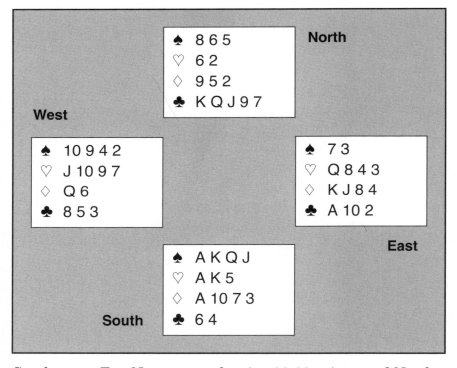

North
♠ 8 6 5
♡ 6 2
◇ 9 5 2
♣ K Q J 9 7

West
♠ 10 9 4 2
♡ J 10 9 7
◇ Q 6
♣ 8 5 3

East
♠ 7 3
♡ Q 8 4 3
◇ K J 8 4
♣ A 10 2

South
♠ A K Q J
♡ A K 5
◇ A 10 7 3
♣ 6 4

South opens Two No-trumps, showing 20-22 points, and North raises to Three No-trumps. West leads the jack of hearts, on which East plays the eight, an encouraging card, as she wants partner to continue hearts when she gets in. The declarer plays the six of clubs to West's three and North's king. Now declarer continues with the queen of clubs. What should East do? Naturally she wants to restrict the declarer to as few club tricks as possible. The key is her partner's play of the three on the first round of clubs. This is clearly her lowest club, as East can see the two. Therefore West has an odd number of clubs. This could be one, but then South has four clubs and will always be able to get to his club tricks. If West has three clubs, however, East should win the second club, as then there is no further entry to the club suit in dummy. East continues hearts, and declarer can only make eight tricks. Note that if she ducks the second club, declarer has nine tricks.

Counting Declarer's Points

Often the declarer has indicated in the bidding a range of points which he has. Invariably he will be telling the truth. You can frequently work out which cards declarer must have or cannot have during the play, if you train yourself to count.

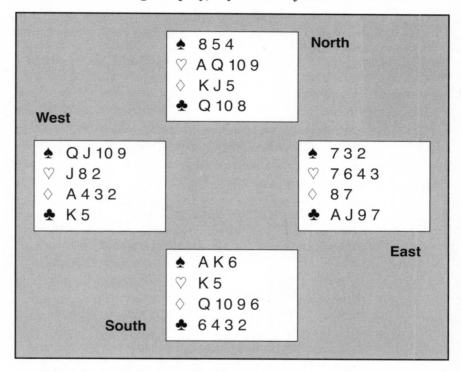

An important aspect of bridge is that one can assign any reasonable range of points to your opening bids or rebids, but you must inform your opponents of your agreements when they ask you. Let us say that North-South have the uncontested auction One No-trump—Two Clubs—Two Diamonds—Three No-trumps. You can ask them, and they must tell you, that they are playing a weak no-trump, showing 12-14 points. They must also tell you, if asked, that Two Clubs is the Stayman convention and Two Diamonds denies a four-card major. You lead the queen of spades as West. Your partner plays the two, which, you may remember, is a discouraging signal in spades. South wins with the ace of spades, and plays a diamond to the king which wins, the jack of diamonds which you allow to hold, and a diamond to the ten, partner discarding the three of hearts. You win with the ace; what do you do next? Well, if you remember partner's signal in spades, you can conclude that South also has the king of spades. He is known to have the queen of diamonds. Partner's three of hearts is also a discouraging signal, so that South must have the king of hearts. If South also has the ace of clubs, he would have 16 points, too many to open One No-trump. Continue with the king of clubs and take four club tricks to defeat the contract.

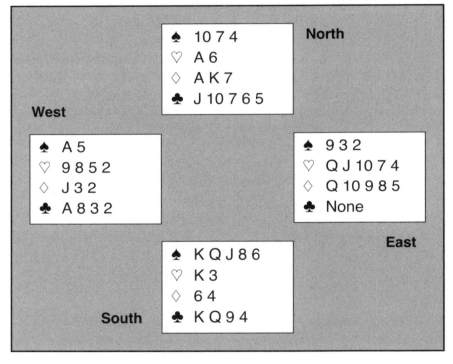

Another example of deducing declarer's hand. The uncontested auction in the above deal, with South dealer, was One Spade—Two Clubs—Three Clubs—Three Spades—Four Spades. West is on lead and can be pretty sure the opponents have at least eight spades and at least eight clubs between them. She should lead the ace of clubs and then give her partner a club ruff. Her partner can have no more than one club. Later when she wins the ace of trumps she gives her partner another club ruff. On any lead other than a club, East will get only one club ruff.

Try it Yourself

Exercise 40: The opponents bid One No-trump —Three No-trumps. What do you lead as West?

♠ Q J 9 6
♡ 7 4
◇ A 8 3
♣ Q J 9 4

West

Exercise 41: South opens One No-trump and all pass. West leads the king of hearts. Dummy plays small. Which card do you play as East?

♠ Q 7
♡ 9 8 5
◇ A 8 7 6
♣ K 7 4 2

North

♠ 10 5 4 3
♡ A 3 2
◇ 9 4 2
♣ A Q 6

East

Exercise 42: The opponents bid One Spade—Three Spades—Four Spades. Partner leads the ace of hearts. Which card do you play as East?

♠ J 10 8 2
♡ 8 7
◇ A 8 7 4
♣ K Q 5

North

♠ Q 5
♡ 9 2
◇ J 9 6 3 2
♣ A 7 6 4

East

Chapter Ten

Simple Conventions and Treatments

- ■ **Negative Doubles**
- ■ **Weak Two Bids**
- ■ **The Gerber Convention**
- ■ **Two-suited Overcalls**
- ■ **The Jump Cue-bid**
- ■ **Transfers**
- ■ **Defences to One No-trump**
- ■ **Try it Yourself**

When you play in a bridge club for the first time, you will come across many bids that you have not read about in this book. You will find opponents tapping the table or waving an alert card to indicate that they are using a conventional bid. The most common reasons for their unusual displays of activity will be covered in this chapter. Don't forget that you can always enquire what their bids mean if you need to know.

Negative Doubles

You will remember that a double of an opening bid at the one-, two- or three-level, or a double when the opponents have opened one of a suit, or opened and responded in a suit, was for take-out, asking partner to bid his best suit. This is because it is rare for your side to have sufficient combined assets to defeat an opposing contract at the one-level. It is also infrequent that you have the strength to defeat the opponents when they overcall at the one- or two-level, and most tournament players do not use a double after an overcall of up to Two Spades as penalties. For example, on page 47 you had the following hand:

♠ K J 6 3
♡ 8 7
♢ K J 4
♣ 10 8 5 2

Partner opened One Heart and the next person overcalled Two Clubs. If you play negative doubles, then you would double on this hand. This is a take-out double which would normally show four cards in the unbid major and at least six points if the overcall is at the one-level, at least eight points if the overcall is at the two-level. Alternatively, some hands with a five- or six-card suit with fewer than ten points would begin with a double, followed by bidding the suit.

Weak Two Bids

In our chapter on opening bids we described the requirements for opening the bidding at the two-level. However, these very strong hands do not occur that often, and many club players use an opening bid of Two Diamonds, Two Hearts and Two Spades to show a weak hand. The purpose of this is to make a pre-emptive bid without risking going to the three-level. This would be an example of an opening bid of Two Hearts using this method:

♠ 8
♡ K Q 10 7 5 3
♢ K 9 4
♣ 10 8 5

Usually (but not always) the bid promises a six-card suit and about 6-10 points. You may decide to take up the method yourself, in which case some of the more advanced books in the Bibliography explain the principles to follow.

If you play rubber bridge only, you will be less likely to meet the weak two-bid, and some clubs may not allow you to use it.

The Gerber Convention

This often overused convention employs the bid of Four Clubs to ask for aces. It should only be used in response to an opening bid of One No-trump or Two No-trumps, as a response of Four No-trumps would then be an invitational bid, not the Blackwood Convention. The responses are as follows:

Four Diamonds	No aces (or four)
Four Hearts	One ace
Four Spades	Two aces
Four No-trumps	Three aces

After the response has been received, a further bid of Five Clubs, by the player who bid Four Clubs, asks for kings, with the responses being the same, but at a level higher.

The inexperienced player is advised not to use this convention just yet, but if you do wish to use it, then you should restrict its use to a direct response of Four Clubs to an opening bid of One No-trump or Two No-trumps. The rest of the time the bid should show clubs, or be a cue-bid.

Two-suited Overcalls

The Unusual No-trump
The overcall of Two No-trumps is usually employed to show a hand with at least five cards in each minor suit (diamonds and clubs), with each suit having at least two honours, and ten or

fewer points. If the opponents have opened One Club or One Diamond, then the two suits shown are the lowest two unbid suits. This would be an example of an overcall of Two No-trumps over an opposing opening bid of One Spade:

♠ J
♡ 8 2
♢ K Q J 9 5
♣ Q J 10 8 4

The above is known as the unusual Two No-trumps. Indeed such an overcall can be incorporated into a wider defensive system by linking it with ...

The Michaels Cue-bid

Using this system, the cue-bid of the suit which your opponent opens, shows ten or more cards in the major suits, or if the suit opened is a major, in the other major plus one of the minors. Again you show fewer than ten points and both suits should have two honours. This would be an acceptable Michaels cue-bid of Two Diamonds over an opposing One Diamond opening:

♠ K J 7 5 8
♡ Q J 6 4 3 2
♢ 9
♣ 2

Partner will usually select his better major. It should be noted that if you have, say, spades and diamonds, and the opponents open One Club, then neither of the above bids is correct. Two Clubs would show both majors, and Two No-trumps would show both red suits. There is a convention which allows you to show the two extreme suits:

Ghestem

This invention of the great French player Pierre Ghestem uses the overcall of Three Clubs to show the highest two unbid suits and the cue-bid to show the other two suits. Two No-trumps again shows the lowest two suits. If, therefore, the opponents open One Diamond, a bid of Three Clubs would show both majors and again fewer than ten points with at least two honours in each suit. As this bid is being made at the three-level, you need two good suits or some extra distribution. This would be an acceptable bid of Three Clubs after an opponent opened the bidding with One Heart:

♠ Q J 10 7 5
♡ None
◇ K J 10 5 3 2
♣ 10 6

There are several versions of Ghestem in use, and, if you play the convention, you must ensure that you are both playing the same method! One other point to make is that although the above two-suited overcalls are normally made on hands with fewer than ten points, you can also use the bids on very strong hands. These are hands which you would open at the two-level, or hands that are likely to make game if one suit is supported.

 TIP: Only used a two-suited overcall on weak hands or very strong hands. On in-between hands make a simple overcall

Of course, with the strong version, you then bid game when partner selects the suit he prefers.

The Jump Cue-bid

A bid of three of the suit opened at the one-level is a special bid which asks your partner to bid Three No-trumps if he or she has a stopper in the suit opened. That stopper must be the ace, the guarded king, the twice guarded queen, or four cards including the jack.

♠ 8
♡ A 7
◇ A K Q J 10 8 4
♣ A 3 2

If an opponent opened One Spade, you would bid Three Spades asking partner to bid Three No-trumps if she has a stopper in spades. Without one, she has to bid Four Clubs and you will bid Four Diamonds on the above hand.

Transfers

If you join a bridge club or intend to play in tournaments, you will soon come across transfer bids. A transfer bid is a request for partner to bid the next suit up, but only in special predetermined situations, almost exclusively after an opening bid in no-trumps. In this book we shall look briefly at major-suit transfers after an opening bid in no-trumps.

Playing transfers, a bid of Two Diamonds in response to One No-trump asks partner to bid Two Hearts. A bid of Two Hearts in response to One No-trump asks partner to bid Two Spades. The person using the transfer can then pass, with a hand that would have made a weak take-out into a major suit, or bid on with a hand with an interest in reaching game. So, transfer bids kill two birds with one stone, but the downside is the loss of the natural bid Two Diamonds, showing a weak hand with diamonds.

In response to an opening bid of Two No-trumps, the structure is the same. A response of Three Diamonds asks partner to bid Three Hearts and a response of Three Hearts asks partner to bid Three Spades. Again the responder can pass, to show a weak hand, or bid on, showing a hand worth game.

Defences to One No-trump

Overcalling on a five-card suit when an opponent opens One No-trump is rather risky. The partner of the player opening One No-trump has a good idea of his partner's points, so can often penalise you with a double. Consequently, two-suited overcalls of One No-trump have become popular worldwide, with the bids of Two Clubs and Two Diamonds showing a two-suited hand and not usually promising the suit bid. One popular method is an overcall of Two Clubs showing both majors, the Landy Convention. You usually promise nine cards in total in the majors (divided 5-4) and about 8-14 points. This hand would qualify for a bid of Two Clubs over an opposing One No-trump:

♠ A Q 6 5
♡ J 10 8 6 3
◇ K 4 2
♣ 8

Partner will normally bid the major he prefers in response. Another convention, known as Asptro, is to use Two Clubs over the opposing One No-trump opening bid to show hearts and another suit and Two Diamonds to show spades and another suit, with the same sort of high-card requirements.

We would recommend that you postpone using either of these methods until you have been playing for a while.

Try it Yourself

Exercise 43: You are playing negative doubles. Your partner opens One Diamond and the next player bids One Spade. What do you bid?

    ♠ K J 6 4
    ♡ 9 8
    ♢ Q 5 3
    ♣ K 10 7 5

Exercise 44: You are using the Gerber Convention. What do you respond to One No-trump on this hand?

    ♠ K Q 4
    ♡ A 2
    ♢ K Q J 10 9 6 4
    ♣ A

Exercise 45: Your right-hand opponent opens One Spade and you are using the Unusual No-trump. What do you bid?

    ♠ 8
    ♡ 9 7
    ♢ J 8 7 6 5
    ♣ Q 8 5 4 3

Exercise 46: Your right-hand opponent opens One Heart and you are not using any conventions. What do you bid?

    ♠ A 2
    ♡ 8
    ♢ A K Q J 10 8 7
    ♣ K Q 5

Exercise 47: You have agreed to use the Landy Defence to One No-trump. What do you overcall on this hand?

    ♠ 8 7
    ♡ A 5 3
    ♢ K 5 4
    ♣ K Q J 7 5

Chapter Eleven

Computers, Videos and the Internet

- ■ **Bridge Computers**
- ■ **Videos**
- ■ **Internet Servers**
- ■ **Internet Sites**
- ■ **Suppliers**
- ■ **Clubs**

The twenty-first century will bring far more opportunities for the bridge player to compete with other players. There is already an Internet World Championship. Programs and videos are available which cover both playing and tuition. There has never been a more exciting or worthwhile time to learn the game.

Bridge Computers

Ten years ago, bridge computers were not strong enough to provide a decent game for the serious bridge player. They were also poor as a learning tool as they often passed forcing bids. As top international Zia Mahmood found when he challenged eight of the world's leading computer programs early in 2000, they have come a long way since then. Many experts believe the best program at the time of writing is:

Ginsberg's Intelligent Bridge (GIB) 4.1. This uses a wide variety of bidding systems and includes more than 9,000 deals from top tournaments, so you can compare your actions with World Champions. You can get hints if you are uncertain of what to do at any point. Learn to Play Bridge software is included. You need a 133 MHz Pentium machine or equivalent with 32 MB RAM.

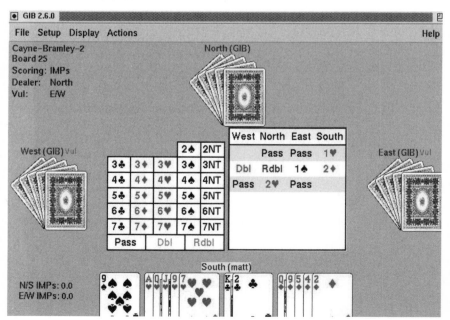

The GIB Interface

A number of other programs are perhaps not as strong as GIB. Those that have features worth mentioning are included below:

Bridge Baron II is available for both PC (again requiring Windows 95 or later with 16 MB RAM) or the Mac or iMac (System 7 or higher, 2MB RAM, 13 inch or larger monitor). It includes a deal generator where you can set parameters, which is useful to practice certain areas of bidding. There is also a conventions program where you can test bidding conventions.

Blue Chip Bridge has a Bidding Tutor which gives advice during the auction and a Playing Tutor to give hints during the play. You can edit the bidding database, take back errors and make a claim of the contract to curtail play when you are sure of success. It requires Pentium II with 32 MB Ram.

Bridge Master Class II is easy to use and has an interactive video tutorial. It is not as strong as the above programs, but is fine for beginners, and is the cheapest of the programs at under £40.

Q Plus 2000 Software had an attractive interface and a very good manual. It offered a choice of eight bidding systems, which will give you flexibility if you meet partners from around the world over the Internet!

Oxford Bridge 6 allowed substantial self-programming of the bidding system and a good manual which explained how to do this. It is more suitable for someone who has been playing a few years. The post-mortem feature is attractive.

All the above require Windows 95 or later.

In addition to the above playing programs, there are a number of tutorial programs, mainly produced in America. The only one really suitable for beginners is:

Learn Bridge which uses excellent multimedia features to teach the game from the start. You can practise bidding, declarer play and defence. It should be noted, however, that this program uses the American '5-card major' system, not the Acol system taught in this book. You need Windows 3.1 or later.

For stronger players:

Bridge Master 2000 provides 180 pre-dealt hands in which you have to find the best line of play. You can try again or ask

Bridge Master to explain the correct line fully. The play problems were of many types and we found them very testing.

As you progress in bridge, you may want to move on to the instructional programs from top US player and teacher Mike Lawrence:

Private Bridge Lessons 1 and **Private Bridge Lessons 2** both cover more difficult aspects of declarer play. These require a 386 with 4MB RAM and Win 3.1 or later.

Finally, the best program for working out correct play in any contract is:

Deep Finesse which uses brute-force methods to establish optimal play for both sides. Again this is only really of benefit for serious tournament players. Requires Windows 95 or later, and 8MB RAM.

Videos

There are many instructional videos which will appeal to those who enjoy learning through this medium.

Play Bridge with Zia is a joint production featuring the charismatic Pakistani/American Zia Mahmood with English lady international Michelle Handley explaining the basics for beginners.

Bridge Masterclass by Tony Forrester is more advanced. Britain's number one player teaches hand valuation, defence, bidding, sacrificing and many other themes in four instructional videos.

Finally, Australian expert **Ron Klinger's Video Series** includes subjects such as card combinations, opening leads, hand valuation and tips on bidding.

All the above programs and videos should be available from the suppliers on page 115. All videos are VHS, European style.

Internet Servers

You can now play bridge 24 hours a day on the Internet and there are several good sites to choose between. Undoubtedly one of the best for the serious player is:

The well-established OKBridge site

OKBridge (www.okbridge.com)

Here you will find top players from all over the world, including the occasional World Champion. You can play with your regular partner or just log on as an individual. The lobby displays all the tables in play and the ability level, form of scoring and bidding system in use. You join a table, ask if you can sit, and are soon under way. Downloading software is easy, and there are many extra features, including a reasonably accurate rating list. There are regular tournaments and a two-tier membership system depending on whether you wish to play in these. Membership is from $100 per year. Occasionally the server crashes, although the blame may lie with the ISP.

EBU Online Club (www.ebuonline.co.uk)

This British based club run by the English Bridge Union has mainly players from the UK, and you will find the majority of the players using a bidding system very similar to the one in this book. You can start at a beginner's table, and we were impressed with the standard of courtesy. You can try the site as a guest for one month, and then membership is £40 per year. There are a number of currently free sites which offer competition against other players. They are of varying quality, and attract a wide range of abilities. The most impressive was:

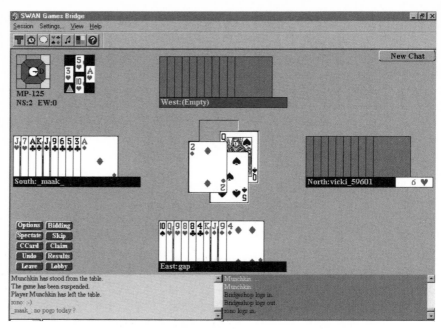

The superbly-designed Swan Games interface

SwanGames (www.swangames.com)

Many different types of events are organised, both social and competitive, and free weekly lessons are offered! The software, designed by Matt Reklaitis, is particularly impressive.

Two large sites are Microsoft Zone at www.zone.com and Yahoo at http://games.yahoo.com.The former 'fills up' half-full tables with computers, so that you always get a game, but the standard of the computers is only mediocre. The latter works well, but on some computers the Java applet may take quite a while to load. Perhaps the smallest site which had only a few tables in play when we logged in was at www.floater.org, but the interface and functions were excellent. A very friendly site at www.pogo.com has typically 800 players on-line. It also offers a wide range of other card and board games. We were also impressed with the interface and professional approach of the site at www.winbridge.net. This is run by Shawn Quinn, who is currently the highest-ranked women bridge player in the world. Another site at www.e-bridgemaster.com holds regular events and also provides vugraph commentary by experts on major bridge tournaments. It was very professional and is also staging challenge matches with commentary by leading players, but now makes an annual charge of $110.

Finally a Dutch/English site at www.stepbridge.net was stated to work, using emulation software, on both a Macintosh and Linux. Possibly other sites do so as well. You may need to ask a sysop (adviser) on Stepbridge for some help, however, as some of the FAQ files were only in Dutch. Finally the well-run Norwegian-based site (in English) at www.topbridge.com, provides individual tournaments with standard bidding.

Internet Sites

The two best places to start if you want to surf bridge on the net are the Bridge World site at www.bridgeworld.com and the Great Bridge Links site at www.greatbridgelinks.com. Both provide a free e-mail newsletter and have comprehensive listings of servers providing online bridge playing, articles of general interest, home pages, federations and a lot more. The latter has a particular good section for Macintosh users. A great variety of material can be found on Richard Pavlicek's site at www.rpbridge.net. It has a wide selection of newspaper columns, interactive puzzles, reviews and well-organised links. Also worth visiting is the bridge section of www.msoworld.com.

The English Bridge Union site at www.ebu.co.uk is well-maintained and always up-to-date. Here you can find results and details of clubs and events in the UK. North American readers will find the site at www.baronbarclay.com of interest. If you want to deal hands conforming to certain specifications, in order to practice bidding, you will find the site at www.playbridge.com of use. Finally, the free newsgroups can be read off-line; rec.games.bridge is the one of most interest.

Suppliers

The following suppliers of bridge equipment, computers and magazines are all recommended and have sites on the Internet where you can buy their products.

Baron Barclay Bridge Supplies, 3600 Chamberlain Lane, Suite 230, Louisville, Kentucky 40241, USA. Tel: (1) 502 426 0410; Fax: (1) 502 426 2044. www.baronbarclay.com

C & T Bridge Supplies, 3838 Catalina Street, Los Alamitos, CA 9070 USA. Tel: (562) 598 7010; Fax: (562) 430 8309.

J W & S Hardy, 63 Tristan Street, Carindale, QLD 4152, Australia. Tel: (61) 7 33988898. www.uq.net.au/~zzjhardy/

Chess & Bridge Centre, 369 Euston Road, London NW1 3AR. Tel: (44) 207 388 2404; Fax: (44) 207 388 2407. www.bridgemagazine.co.uk; email: bridgeshop@easynet.co.uk

Bridge Plus, P O Box 384, Reading RG1 5YP. Tel/Fax: (44) 118 9351052. www.bridge-plus.co.uk; email: bridgeplus@patrol.i-way.co.uk

Bridge Today, Griffin Enterprises, 3329 Spindletop Dr NW, Kennesaw, GA 30144-7336, USA. www.bridgetoday.com; email: gran@netvision.net.il

The Bridge World. P O Box 299, Scarsdale, NY10583-2099, USA. www.bridgeworld.com; email: mail@bridgeworld.com

Mr Bridge, Ryden Grange, Bisley, Surrey GU12 2TH. Tel: (44) 1483 489961; Fax: (44) 1483 797302. www.mrbridge.co.uk

Many of the above produce or distribute a bridge magazine and all should send you a catalogue of their products.

Clubs

There are full details of clubs in all of the affiliated members of the World Bridge Federation on the Internet. The major English speaking governing bodies are as follows:

American Contract Bridge League, 2990 Airways Boulevard, Memphis TN 38116-3847 USA. Tel: (1) 901 332 5586. Fax: (1) 901 332 5594. www.acbl.org

Australian Bridge Federation, P O Box 397, Fyshwick, ACT 2509, Australia. Tel: (02) 6239 2265. Fax: (02) 6239 1816. www.abf.com.au

Canadian Bridge Federation, 2719 East Jolly Place, Regina SK, S4V0X8. Tel: (306) 761 1677; Fax: (306) 789 4919. www.cbf.ca

English Bridge Union, Broadfields, Bicester Road, Aylesbury HP19 8AZ. Tel: (01206) 317200; Fax: (01296) 394414. www.ebu.co.uk

There are four federations in the UK, covering England, Scotland, Wales and Ireland. Contact details for their secretaries can be found at www.ecatsbridge.com.

Scoring

The scoring is an important aspect of the game, but you are allowed to use an *aide memoire* and, indeed, basic bridge scorecards are included in many packs of cards. It does look professional, however, if you know how to score. The English International, leading bridge commentator and trainer, David Burn, always impresses his team-mates with his speed of scoring. His speed of bridge analysis is not bad either!

There are two main types of bridge, rubber bridge and duplicate bridge, and the scoring is different in each:

Rubber Bridge

This is the most common form of the game when played at home or in small groups and requires very little organisation and only four players. A rubber concludes when one partnership makes the equivalent of two game contracts.

Making a contract

If you make a contract you score the following points:

In clubs or diamonds, 20 points for each level that you called. In hearts or spades, 30 points for each level that you called. In no-trumps, 40 points for the first level and 30 points for each subsequent level that you bid.

So, if you make Three Clubs, you score 3 x 20 = 60 points.

All the points for bidding and making contracts are scored **below the line** which means that they count towards your target of 100 points which gives you a game.

Once you reach a total of 100 points you draw a line and start play towards a new game. The points the opponents have below the line in the previous game do not count towards the next game. A partnership that has made one game in that rubber is said to be vulnerable, and this can affect the scoring of subsequent hands. If they have not yet made a game contract they are said to be non-vulnerable. The rubber is the best of three games and when you achieve this target a bonus is added to your score. This is as follows:

500 for winning two games to the opponents' one

700 for winning two games to the opponents' none

You can also score points above the line in several ways:

Overtricks

These are scored above the line and are 20 for each overtrick in clubs and diamonds and 30 for each overtrick in hearts, spades or no-trumps.

Making Doubled and Redoubled Contracts

If you make a doubled or redoubled contract, then you first enter double or quadruple the points for the contract you bid below the line. If that brings your total over 100 points, then you have made a game and draw a line again. You also score a bonus above the line for making a doubled or redoubled contract of 50 or 100 points respectively. In addition, any overtricks you make are scored above the line, as follows:

For non-vulnerable doubled overtricks	100 each
For vulnerable doubled overtricks	200 each
For non-vulnerable redoubled overtricks	200 each
For vulnerable redoubled overtricks	400 each

Penalties

If the declarer fails in a contract, then penalties are awarded:

a) Non-vulnerable, 50 points for each trick by which you fail.

b) Vulnerable, 100 points for each trick by which you fail.

c) If you are doubled or redoubled then the penalties increase dramatically according to this table:

	1 Down	2 Down	3 Down	4 Down
Non-vulnerable	100	300	500	800
Vulnerable	200	500	800	1100

After that both rows increase by 300 points for each trick that you go down, so be careful not to bid too high — the opponents can double you and reap a rich reward!

The penalty for going down in a redoubled contract is easy to calculate; you work out the penalty if the contract were doubled, and then double that.

Slam Bonuses

There are four slam bonuses, depending on whether you bid and make 12 tricks (small slam) or 13 tricks (grand slam) and whether or not you are vulnerable:

Non-vulnerable small slam	500
Vulnerable small slam	750
Non-vulnerable grand slam	1000
Vulnerable grand slam	1500

You only score the slam bonus for the level that you call. So if you make two overtricks in Four Spades, you do not score the slam bonus. You do not increase the slam bonuses if the contract was doubled or redoubled.

Honours

If, in any one hand, whether declarer, dummy or a defender, you have the five top trumps in a suit contract you get a bonus of 150 points, or 100 points for any four of the five. In a no-trump contract you get 150 points for the four aces. These honours are only awarded in rubber bridge.

Duplicate Bridge

In duplicate bridge the cards are taken from a duplicate wallet and played in front of you, and not gathered by the partnership winning the trick. At the end of the hand, the number of tricks made is entered on a scoresheet and each player's hand is put back in the duplicate wallet, which has four slots, one for each player. When you play duplicate bridge, you and your partner are competing against the other pairs who will hold your cards.

As each hand is a separate entity there are no scores above and below the line, just one score for each hand. Obviously there are no bonuses for making a rubber either, but the scores for tricks made are the same as in rubber bridge. Also, each successful contract gets a bonus as follows:

For making any part-score contract	50 points
For making a non-vulnerable game	300 points
For making a vulnerable game	500 points

So, if you bid Two Hearts and make one overtrick, you would score 60 + 30 + 50 = 140.

In addition the bonuses for making a slam are added to those for making a game, so that bidding and making Six Hearts, vulnerable, without any overtricks, would score 180 + 500 + 750 = 1430 points.

The addition for overtricks, and for making doubled or redoubled contracts is the same, as is the penalty conceded.

Chicago Scoring

In Chicago you are playing rubber bridge, but you do not play a rubber. Instead you play a set number of hands, invariably a multiple of four. The score recorded each time is the same as for duplicate bridge. In some clubs part scores carry forward to the next hand and in others overtricks are not scored at all.

Pairs Scoring

When a pair takes part in an event, such as the weekly duplicate bridge tournament at the local club, the scores will be recorded on a travelling scoresheet which accompanies each duplicate board. Each pair will score on any board:

One point for each pair that they did better than, plus

Half a point for each pair that they did the same as, but

No points for each pair that they did worse than.

So, for a board that was played nine times, a pair can get a score between 0 and 8, inclusive. After all the boards, typically 24, are scored, each pair will receive a percentage. The winning percentage may be around 60% with the last place scoring 40%.

Teams Scoring

There are World Championships for pairs, but bridge at the very highest level is mainly a team game. In a team event, there are four members of a team (or a multiple of four on occasions). Two members of the team play the North-South cards and two members play the East-West cards. Again a duplicate board is used to ensure that exactly the same hand is played by both pairs of the team. The score achieved by the North-South pair is then compared with the score conceded by the East-West pair, and the difference is usually converted into International Match Points (IMPs), on a scale which runs from 1-25. This form of scoring can also be used for pairs events, where the scores by each pair are compared and the difference from the average or 'datum' is converted into IMPs. Indeed the two methods of scoring most prevalent in competitions on the many Internet servers are pairs and teams scoring.

Other scoring methods include point-a-board, where the team doing better on the board wins one point, and aggregate scoring, where total points scored are simply added. The latter is less popular as it gives undue weighting to, say, a grand slam that makes luckily or fails unluckily.

Solutions to Exercises

1 a) The last bid, 1C, was not high enough and is not allowed because clubs ranks below no-trumps.

   b) The final bid, 2S, is allowed, even though 1S would have been high enough.

   c) The final bid, 3NT, is permitted because three is higher than two.

   d) The final bid, 1NT, is not allowed because the previous bid was at the two-level.

2 a) queen of diamonds.

   b) two of hearts.

   c) eight of clubs.

   d) ten of diamonds.

3 a) queen of hearts.

   b) six of hearts.

   c) queen of clubs.

   d) two of hearts.

4 Correct is c) after the opening lead has been made.

5 a) is true; b) is false, and is the only occasion that the auction does not end with three consecutive passes; c) is false; the highest call is Seven No-trumps which means that you need to take thirteen tricks; d) is true.

6 The hand has 13 points and the correct opening bid is One Heart, the longest suit.

7 The correct bid is to pass. The hand has only three high-card points.

8 You have 12 points and should overcall Two Clubs. The suit is strong enough to bid at the two-level.

9 The correct bid on the hand is to pass. You have 11 points and a five-card suit, but the opponents have opened One Heart, which is your best suit. You just pass and await developments.

10 The correct bid is Two Spades. To overcall at the two-level shows 12 points and a good five-card suit or 10 points and a six-card suit.

11 The correct opening bid is One Spade. Including distribution you have 13 points, and should open the higher of two five-card suits.

12 Despite having five clubs, the right opening bid is One No-trump, showing a balanced hand of 12-14 points.

13 The correct opening bid is One Club. You have three four-card suits, and with a red singleton should open the suit below the singleton.

14 This hand is much too strong for a pre-emptive bid and you should open One

Diamond. Including distribution you have 14 points.

15   You have 25 points, plus one for distribution, and should open Two Clubs, the artificial bid showing 23 or more points.

16   This is an awkward hand, but you have 13 points including distribution. You should start with Three Spades, a forcing bid. If partner now bids Three No-trumps, however, you should pass, as you are unlikely to be able to make Five Diamonds, so should not introduce your diamonds at the four-level.

17   You have to respond One Spade. You do not have enough points to bid Two Clubs. The nightmare scenario is partner rebidding Two Diamonds, but you will just have to pass that before things get even worse!

18   The correct response is One Heart. Even though your spade suit is better than your heart suit, you should still start with the lower of two four-card suits as responder.

19   The correct response is to raise partner to Three Spades. Partner cannot pass this, even though you may have quite a poor hand. Your first step is to show the spade support. If you bid Four Spades you would be showing a weaker hand.

20   You should just pass here. If partner has a seven-card club suit headed by the ace and queen, you will still only make eight tricks in Three No-trumps against opponents who are good defenders. It is unreasonable to expect partner to have anything in addition to that, and he may easily have a little less!

21   With this hand we recommend that you pass. You have nine points, but none of them are in spades. The holdings in the red suits are particularly unattractive.

22   This is a normal take-out double, even though you have 15-17 points. It is better to double when you have only two of opener's suit and at least three cards in the other three suits.

23   The correct bid is to double, showing 16 or more points.

24   Now we overcall One No-trump, showing 15-17 points.

25   As we have decided our jump overcalls show a weak hand, this is ideal for a jump overcall of Three Clubs, showing at least a six-card suit headed by two honours and 6-10 points.

26   The correct bid is to raise to Two No-trumps. This shows 17-18 points. If partner has 8-9 points he will bid game, with seven he will have to decide. Note that partner can now bid Three Hearts if she has three-card heart support.

27   The right bid is to raise partner to Three Diamonds. This shows 12-14 points and four-card support for partner. This is a much more descriptive choice than the rebid of Two Spades.

28   Here it looks right to raise partner to Two Spades, but this would be a serious underbid. You have 14 high-card points including two points for 6-4 shape, plus three shortage points for a doubleton plus singleton, a total of 17 points. You are worth a raise to Three Spades. If partner has a hand something like ♠ KJ92 ♡ 54 ◇ Q54 ♣ Q732, you would expect to make Four Spades, losing one spade, one diamond and one club.

29   This is a slightly awkward hand, but the best rebid is Two No-trumps, showing 18-19 points. The most likely game contract at the moment is Three No-trumps, and you have a fairly balanced hand. The alternative rebid of Three Clubs shows about 15-17 points, and is therefore an underbid.

30   You should bid Two Hearts, a reverse bid, as you are bidding a higher-ranking suit than your first one at the two-level. This promises 16 or more points.

31   The correct bid is Two No-trumps, showing 12-14 points. Note that this is somewhat stronger than a Two No-trump response to an opening bid, as partner's overcall is only assumed to have ten points.

32   You have a poor hand, only just enough to respond in the first place. You should, however, bid Two Hearts which just says that you prefer hearts to diamonds. Even though you have two of each, partner bid hearts first, so he is sure to have at least as many hearts as diamonds, and quite likely to have longer hearts.

33   It looks tempting to raise to Three Clubs, but partner can pass this. As you have 16 points including distribution, you want to be in game. You should therefore bid Two Diamonds, the fourth suit. This is an artificial forcing bid, and partner will continue the bidding until game is reached.

34   You have a great hand, just short of opening a strong Two Spades. You should now make a cue-bid of Four Clubs, showing the ace or a void in that suit. You hope partner can respond with a cue-bid of Four Diamonds. Note that the hand is unsuitable for Four No-trumps, the Blackwood Convention, because it has a void.

35   Again you would like to raise diamonds, but whichever level you raise, partner may pass. You probably want to be in a slam here, as you have 19 points including distribution, and partner has opened. Again bid Two Spades, the fourth suit, which is artificial and forcing. Partner will bid again, and you can then support diamonds and partner will know you have a good hand. A simpler approach, and one we would favour if you are just starting out in bridge, is to bid Six Diamonds immediately. This is likely to be your best contract, even though we would not be at all surprised if you could make Seven Diamonds.

36   The correct line is to duck the opening lead in both hands. If the opponents continue spades, you can win the second or third round of the suit, and then take the diamond finesse. Assuming that North has at least three spades, if South wins the king of diamonds, and has a third spade to play, you will only lose three spade tricks and one diamond trick.

37   The right play is again to duck the opening lead. You should then be able to ruff a club in the dummy before drawing the trumps. You will thus score the ace of clubs, a club ruff, five trumps and three spades. Alternative plans risk South gaining the lead too soon and are much less safe.

38   Here you cannot afford to play trumps immediately, or the defence will surely cash two club tricks. The correct line is to win the club lead and to take the spade finesse, even though you have a singleton. If it holds you can throw a club loser on the ace of spades and then play trumps. If it loses you will go two down, but the risk is worthwhile.

39   This is just a case of counting your tricks. If you play a heart at trick two, you will make two spades, two hearts and five diamonds. If instead you play on clubs, you will usually be too slow and the defence will establish enough spade tricks first.

40   The correct lead is the queen of spades, the top of a sequence. You have a very similar holding in clubs, and the queen of clubs is the second choice. However, when you are leading against no-trumps, and the opponents have not bid a major suit or used the Stayman Convention, you should prefer to lead a major instead of a minor.

41   The correct play is to overtake the king of hearts and to return the three of hearts. Partner has the king, queen and either the jack or ten of hearts. She will therefore win at least four heart tricks. If you play the three, partner may think you are playing a discouraging card and may well lead a spade next which you do not want.

42   The correct card to play is the nine of hearts, an encouraging card, even though you do not have a high card in hearts. Partner will then continue with the king of hearts, and a third heart. You will be able to ruff higher than dummy, and you are almost certain to then make your ace of clubs.

43   It is not right to make a negative double on this hand. That would show four of the unbid major, hearts. The correct bid is One No-trump, showing 6-9 points with a stopper in spades.

44   This hand is ideal for the Gerber convention. If partner has two aces, you will continue with Five Clubs, asking for kings. If partner has one king as well, then you will be able to count 13 certain tricks and you will bid Seven No-trumps. Otherwise you can stop at a lower level, depending on partner's response.

45   This hand is too weak and the suits much too poor to use the Unusual No-trump. The correct bid is to pass, even if you are not vulnerable.

46   Even though you are not using any conventions, the bid of Three Hearts would ask any reasonably experienced player to bid Three No-trumps with a heart stopper. You may be skating on thin ice, though, if you try this with a beginner!

47   As you are using the Landy defence to One No-trump, you cannot bid Two Clubs over One No-trump on this hand. That would show both majors, which you do not have. The only alternative is to pass, as a jump to Three Clubs shows a stronger hand than this in terms of playing strength.

Bibliography

There are many thousands of bridge books in print. This book has, of necessity, only covered the basics of the game, and there are many fine books which will take the reader up to the level of a strong tournament player. A series of Bridge Plus booklets covers different aspects of bidding and play. The following six would be the author's recommendation to read next:

Practice Your Stayman by Townsend

Practice Your Opening Leads by Hackett and Hackett

Practice Your Counting by Roth

Practice Your Finessing by Cashmore

Practice Your Signalling by Rigal

Practice Your Fourth-Suit Forcing by Magee

The English Bridge Union has also produced a series of books which are geared towards the improving player. The titles so far are:

Really Easy Bidding

Really Easy Play in No-trumps

Really Easy Mistakes

Really Easy Practice 1

Really Easy Practice 2

All are available from the EBU at the address on page 116.

A couple of other beginner books are also recommended:

Bridge for Beginners by Zia Mahmood

Basic Bridge by Ron Klinger

Finally the keen student may wish to read a number of excellent elementary books on different aspects of bidding, play and defence:

First Principles of Card Play by Marston

Conventional Biding Explained by North

Opening Leads in Bridge by Sowter

Bread-and-Butter Bidding by Senior

Bridge with Brunner by Brunner

Guide to Better Acol Bridge by Klinger

Finally, *50 Bridge Puzzles* by Lamford starts with easy puzzles but progresses to more difficult problems which will test all players.

Bidding Chart

Points	Action
0-1	Usually you pass at each opportunity. You will, however, respond to any two-level opening bid, other than Two No-trumps. If partner opens Two Clubs and rebids Two No-trumps you can pass. You can also make a weak take-out of partner's One No-trump opening bid and you respond to a take-out double unless you wish to defend. You should also bid a five-card or longer suit if partner doubles One No-trump.
2-3	Usually you pass at each opportunity. You will, however, respond to any two-level opening bid, other than Two No-trumps. You can also make a weak take-out of partner's One No-trump opening bid and you respond to a take-out double unless you wish to defend. You should also bid a five-card or longer suit if partner doubles One No-trump. You will bid after a Two No-trump rebid following a Two Club opener.
4-5	Again pass if partner opens at the one-level, unless you have extra support points which allow you to bid. You should respond to all two-level opening bids including Two No-trumps. You can make a weak take-out if partner opens One No-trump. If partner doubles One No-trump you usually pass. Again you usually respond to a take-out double with your best suit. You can open with a pre-emptive bid with a seven-card suit.
6-7	You must now respond to your partner's opening bid, either at the one-level in a new suit, with One No-trump, or by raising partner one level. You respond to all two-level opening bids. If partner opens One No-trump, you can again make a weak take-out. If partner makes a take-out double, you respond in your best suit unless you want to defend. If partner doubles One No-trump you usually pass. If you have a seven-card suit, you can open with a pre-emptive bid.

8-9   Again you must respond to your partner's opening bid, either at the one-level in a new suit, with One No-trump or by raising partner one level. You respond to all two-level opening bids. If partner opens One No-trump you can again make a weak take-out. If partner makes a take-out double, you usually jump a level in your best suit unless you want to defend. If partner doubles One No-trump you usually pass. If you have a good suit you can make an overcall at the one-level. Again you can open with a pre-emptive bid with a seven-card suit. You can also make a weak jump overcall if you have a six-card suit and the oppponents open at the one-level.

10-11   You usually pass if your partner has not opened, but you can make an overcall at the one-level or two-level, the latter with a six-card suit. If you have extra distributional points. you may open the bidding. If partner makes a take-out double you normally jump a level in a new suit, sometimes two levels depending on the hand. If partner opens One No-trump, you usually pass, but you can make a weak take-out or even raise to Two No-trumps, or use the Stayman Convention with 11 points. You can respond at the one- or two-level to an opening bid. You can also respond Two No-trumps or raise partner to three of his suit.

12-14   You can always open the bidding. If you have a balanced hand you open One No-trump; if not you open One of a Suit and rebid a new suit or raise partner. If partner opens One No-trump you can raise to game, bid Stayman, or bid a new suit at the three-level. With 12 points and no five-card suit you raise One No-trump to Two No-trumps. You can still respond at the one- or two-level in a new suit, or bid Three No-trumps in response to an opening bid (only Two No-trumps with 12). If you have four-card support for partner you usually bid a new suit first before raising. If partner makes a take-out double you can bid game or cue-bid the opponent's suit.

15-17	You open at the one-level in your longest suit and rebid One No-trump if you are balanced. You can jump rebid in a six-card suit or raise partner one or two levels as appropriate (usually one level with 15 and two levels with 17; with 16 it depends on the hand). If partner responds at the two-level in a new suit, you rebid Two No-trumps. With 15 points and a balanced hand you can respond Three No-trumps. You can double an opening bid of One No-trump. If partner opens the bidding, you usually just bid your best suit, but you can jump in a new suit with a suitable hand. You can rebid a new suit at the one- or two-level, but if it is at the two-level in a higher-ranking suit than your first, you need 16 points.
18-19	You open at the one-level in your best suit and rebid Two No-trumps if you are balanced. You can also jump in a new suit or raise partner to game if partner responds in a major suit at the one-level. If partner responds at the two-level in a new suit, you rebid Two No-trumps, which forces partner to bid again. If partner opens the bidding, you usually just bid your best suit, but you can jump in a new suit.
20-22	If you have a balanced hand then open Two No-trumps. If you have a hand suitable for opening two of a suit then do so; otherwise open at the one-level. If partner responds you will need to jump rebid in a new suit, or rebid Two No-trumps if partner responds at the two-level. It is important to make a forcing bid if partner does respond.
23-24	You open Two Clubs and then rebid Two No-trumps, if balanced, or your best suit if not.
25-27	You open Two Clubs and then rebid Three No-trumps, if balanced, or two of your best suit if not.
28+	You will not get such hands very often, but if you do, we suggest you take up rubber bridge for money! Open Two Clubs and rebid Four No-trumps, if balanced, or your best suit if not.

In each case you should look at the relevant chapter for more detail.-